Do You Have

FAITH

GOD

in

PLAN

Are We Passing
God Tests Of Faith?

REV. FRANK CHARLESTON JR

AuthorHouse™
1663 Liberty Drive
Bloomington, IN 47403
www.authorhouse.com
Phone: 1 (800) 839-8640

*Scripture quotations marked KJV are from the Holy Bible, King James Version (Authorized Version). First published
in 1611. Quoted from the KJV Classic Reference Bible, Copyright © 1983 by The Zondervan Corporation.*

Published by AuthorHouse 05/26/2015

ISBN: 978-1-5049-0792-7 (sc)
ISBN: 978-1-5049-0793-4 (e)

Print information available on the last page.

*Any people depicted in stock imagery provided by Thinkstock are models,
and such images are being used for illustrative purposes only.
Certain stock imagery © Thinkstock.*

This book is printed on acid-free paper.

*Because of the dynamic nature of the Internet, any web addresses or links contained in this book may have changed
since publication and may no longer be valid. The views expressed in this work are solely those of the author and do not
necessarily reflect the views of the publisher, and the publisher hereby disclaims any responsibility for them.*

authorHOUSE®

DEDICATION

To my Family: I love you all very much

To Christ Blessed Church: Thanks to you all so very much for believe in me and my family.

INTRODUCTION

This book is written for more than one reason. First reason is to let everyone know about God tests, and his plans for our life. Most people don't know or believe that they will go to hell. But most people believe that if they live any kind of way they will still go to heaven, but we must pass most of God tests to get into heaven. Remember and understanding that God love us so much He will help us to get what we have worked for our whole life, heaven or hell. So remember every Christian will have bad days, but is only a test. How is our faith in God? Are we passing today? Think hard before you answer. But remember this world belongs to God, not Satan and Satan is not about to rule over what belongs to God. But! Some people believe that Satan is ruling over the earth and the universe, not so, everything belongs to God. Look these tests will stop when we die out of this world, will our choice be heaven are hell? God is given us the opportunity to pass His tests, The Bible is the only book that can compare with this book. Some things in this book we will not understand, but when the Lord sees us following His instructions, He will help us understand this book. The more we read this book the more we will understand. As we read this book just take a long look at our self to see if we are passing. Christ Blessed Church is asking these questions. Do we not know about God tests? We will be taken these test our whole life. Do we really have all faith in God plans today? Think about it as you read this book. Remember it's only a test, are we passing? Are we following God plans or someone else plan for our life? Remember things of this world is passing away, we must go by God plan. Think about it before you answer. This is about the beginning, how things got started, thing that have happen and things to come.

THE BOOK OF GENESIS

{The book of Genesis is one book of the law in the bible. So study it well for a better understanding. This book is inspired by God and some scriptures of the King James Version of the bible and other interpretations from God through me. All writing in RED is words of Jesus Christ. This book is inspired by God for everyone who doesn't want to go to hell. Look and see what will happen if we don't pass God tests in our life time. There will be weeping, wailing and grinding of teeth and burning for ever and ever and never burning up, think about it! There shall be pain and torment for those unsaved and those left behind. But money can't save us. Everything in this book will help us pass God tests. Remember! People love money more than they love God. But all these scriptures in this book is inspired by God. Study your bible and ask God to help you to understand, He will if we are for real. Remember please don't wait too long; because when we get sick it will be too late. The next breathe maybe our last. The following scripture will help us in pass God tests of faith. This book will not change the bible, but it will help clarify what we read in the bible, our tests begin the day we was born and it will end the day we die. Everything from here on will help us to pass God tests of our faith. Remember God is the examiner of these tests so we will not be able to copy. The church is a place to get prepare for heaven. Heaven is a place for prepare people. Look everyone perception of God is wrong. God is a sprit; so we must worship him in the spirit. It's all about our faith and not about our denominations. It's all about our faith and belief. So remember it's all about your faith and devotion to our God. But if we're not prepared when we die we will go to hell. Are we really passing God test today? What if He came right now; will we be ready for heaven or hell? Your choice}

TIME IS RUNNING OUT

"For the Lord him self shall descend from heaven with a shout, with the voice of the archangel, and with the trump of God: and the dead in Christ shall rise first. 1 TH.4:16 are we passing some of His tests today? Do you believe in the following Scripture? "But the Lord is faithful, who shall establish you, and keep you from evil."2th.3:3. {What do you think: are we passing God tests of faith? We have time for every thing but God, but don't forget time is running out. Look around see our hair is turning gray, our teeth is falling out, we can't run or walk as fast anymore, our father, mother, sisters and brothers will leave us but God will never leave us, we will always leave him. But he will come one day to judge us, will we be ready are not? I'm asking again are we following most of God plan for us in life? Think about it; I'm just one crying out in the wilderness sayings get right and let's go home, are we ready? Think about it.

If we don't get right now and follow God plan we will go to hell. Repent now and come to the Lord while it is time for night come when no man can work? But He will save us from hell, if we are following most of his instructions. We can give everything time, but we can't give God one hour out of seven days. Look God gives us six day to do anything we like to do, but on day seven we can find any excuse for not going to church. Are we passing God tests? In this book we will see three symbols, this one ("") meaning these scriptures are inspired by God in the bible. The second symbol will be the words of Jesus in red and the third symbol {} mean inspired by God through me to be a guideline for us through the bible in this book. All three symbols are to help us to understand now much God love us. I fear God so much because if we desire to go to hell, He will let us go. We must have faith and fear in God. We will have good and bad days but remember all days are God plan for us. Listen to this example scripture it will help us to understand.} "Man that is born of a woman is of few days, and full of trouble."Job.14:1. {But remember he is coming! Are we passing? Please reference to the bible to understand about this book, this is also authority by God as a guide through our life and the bible. These scriptures are inspiration by the Lord, through the King James Bible and through this book, as a guideline for the readers in this book.}

SCRIPTURE WILL HELP US THOUGHTOUT OUR LIFE WITH PRAY

{This book is also written to let everyone know that there is a possibility that they will go to hell; again most people believe that if they live any kind of way they will still go to heaven. We must pass God tests and ask for His forgive. But remember and understand that God love us so much, He will help us to get where we desire to go, heaven or hell. Remember do not allow our self to forget the power of pray. God will hear us through prays. Always remember we can communication with God, but look at the scripture below it will help us to understand what Jesus wants us to do. *"Pray without ceasing."*1TH.5:17. {Those three little words meaning: pray mean to talk to God not man, so pray silent so man can't hear you, without mean non stop, and the words ceasing mean we should never stop praying silent to God. He already knows what we need, so keep that communication open with Him. Some people need scripture to help them to understand, so if you see a lot of scriptures maybe they are not for you, but for someone who need them.} *"And it shall come to pass, that before they call, I will answer; and while they are yet speaking, I will hear."*Isa.65:24. {Praying invites Jesus to act on our behalf. God will replace our desires with his desires. God clean us through a transformation, the renewing of our mind. Consequently when we change our mind, our heart changes and therefore we are able to understand} "And He will come and maybe we will begin to realize the impact of prayer, and start changing thing in our life through prayers. If we confess to God with our heart, He will be faithful and will forgive us. Remember we were dead but look: *"And I saw the dead small and great, stand before God; and the books were opened: and another book was opened, which is the book of life: and the dead were judged out of those things which were written in the books, according to their works. And the sea gave up the dead who were in it; and death and hell delivered up the dead who were in them: and they were judged every man according to their works. And death and hell were cast into the lake of fire. This is the second death. And whosoever was not found written in the book of life was cast into the lake of fire"* Rev.20:12-15. {Remember ever Christian has good and bad days, but is only a test of our faith in God, are we passing? But remember this world and the universe belongs to God, it's not Satan to rule over. Some people believe that Satan is ruling over the earth and the universe, not so everything belongs to God. These tests will stop the day you die. Will we make the right choice? Remember God is given us the opportunity to pass his tests, read the following scriptures below it will help us to understand} *"I must work the works of Him that sent me, while it is day: the night cometh, when no men can work. As long as I am in the world, I am the light of the world."* Joh.9:4-5. {So we must work for God as long as we are alive, for night cometh meaning we die, we can't work. But we will be judge by God. Think about it now are we proclaiming the gospel to the people, read the following scripture it will help us to understand} *"Not forsaking the assembling of ourselves together, as the manner of some is; but exhorting one another: so much the more, as ye see the day approaching"* Heb.10:25. {Do we really understand what Jesus is saying? We can't get to heaven without assembling ourselves together with a church. But if we have not been attending church before we became ill, it will be too late after we become ill. There isn't another way we can go to heaven without going to church. But if you were a regular attendance before you got sick, and kept your faith in God and not in man; you can still get into heaven. But look if we were born mentally ill and unable to understand, yes you can go to heaven, but if we just don't attend church we can't get into heaven. But if we just forgive people and go to church and live according to God plan you will go to heaven. Remember we can't lie to the Lord, He will know when we are lying to him. Jesus did say assembling ourselves together in His name and He would be in the midst. We much have been a church gore, to assembling ourselves together with other faithful people that have a good report with the Lord, when we became ill, not just anyone will do. The scriptures below will help us to understand what God want of pastors.} *"Preaches the word; be instant in season, out of season; reprove, rebuke, exhort with all longsuffering and doctrine. For the time will come when they will not endure sound doctrine; but after their own lusts shall they heap to themselves teachers, having itching ears;"* 2Ti.4:2-3. Preacher, we need to preach God words, not our on words, some preachers preach just for money, or for fable, but we need to get back to God words, and follow His plan at all times. Pastors remember we are just God mail carriers, we are not God. He is not a part time God; He is a full time God. We can't substitute anything for God. God doesn't need us at anytime for anything. The following scripture below will help us to understand a little about God.} *"Study to show thyself approved unto God, a workman that needed not to be ashamed, rightly dividing the word of truth."*2Ti.2:15. {If we do this and follow God instructions, preaching and teaching the right doctrine, we will not fail God tests and go to hell. God will hold us accountable for our teaching the wrong doctrine to his people by sent us to hell. Remember God is not a game; so be sure of your calling read the following} "For many are called, but few are chosen."Matt.22:14. {Today we have a choice heavens or hell? Remember this book will help us to pass God tests, but is will also help us to understand God plan for us, this book will help us know whether or not we are passing God tests, thinking about it before you answer, remember these scriptures they will help us.} "Wherefore I say unto you, All manner of sin and blasphemy shall be forgiven unto men: but the blasphemy against the Holy Ghost shall not be forgiven unto men" "And whosoever speaketh a word against the Son of man, it shall be forgiven him: but whosoever speaketh against the Holy Ghost, it shall not be forgiven him, neither in this world, neither in the world to come." Matt.12:31-32. {Let's look at the meaning of blasphemy: the act of cursing, God slandering, reviling or showing contempt or lack of reverence for God. Read the following scripture it we help us to understand.} "Christians are commanded to avoid behavior that blasphemes the Lord's name and teaching" 1Tim.6:1. {Remember this mean to think about things before we react, sometime we sin over and over again, by reacting before we think. But now pay close attention to the following scriptures and see, if we of passing or not? Jesus believes in us always, but we always disappoint him and let him down. In this book we will see many examples. Remember Noah preached, one hundred and twenty years, the same thing over and over again. Remember it all up to us heaven or hell; it's our choice make is a good one. Reflecting back I can remember when people loved one another, but not today it's all about what I have, competing with one another, not caring about the family God want to see together. The family love for one another is not there any more. Are we passing God little tests? God it not expecting us to be perfect, but He is expecting us to be the best we can be. If we just listen to God and follow His words we just may learn something. We need to lead by learning these three scriptures; they will help us to receive salvation and invite other to be saved. To follow God plan read the scriptures below. These scriptures will help us to learn the Roman Road. Think about it as we read, to learn read seven time a day for seven days.} "As it is written, there is none righteous, no, not one:" "They are all gone out of the way, they are together become unprofitable; there is none that doeth good, no, not one. "Rom 3:10" {Remember what the scriptures said no one, not even you do you understand? But remember we need to follow God plan everyday, but remember God doesn't need our help at anytime?} "For all have sinned, and come short of the glory of God; "Rom.3:23." {That mean there is no special person to God, but we much love God in our heart, remember God have a plan are we passing?} "For the wages of sin is death; but the gift of God is eternal life through

Jesus Christ our Lord." **Rom.6:23**. {He has given us our whole life to get it right, remember it's all up to us and think about that. God will help us to go where ever we choose to go; hell or heaven, are we following God instruction? Look at what God did for us}"But God commended his love toward us, in that, while we were yet sinners, Christ died for us. "**Rom.5:8**." {Jesus did it's all for us; it's time to make a change, have we made the right choose? think about it.} That if thou shall confess with thy mouth the Lord Jesus, and shall believe in thins heart that God hath raised him from the dead, thou shall be saved." For with the heart man believeth unto righteousness; and with the mouth confession is made unto salvation." For whosoever shall call upon the name of the Lord shall be saved." **Rom.10:9, 10, 13**. {If we believe in our heart we can be saved right now and have that faith then we can make heaven our choice. But will we make that right choice before we die? Are we calling upon the name of the Lord in our heart and mouth, we much do both in orders to pass; are we? Think about this :} "Study to shew thyself approved unto God, a workman that needeth not be ashamed, rightly dividing the word of truth": **2Tim 2:15**. {Are we following God instructions studying our bible? It will help us as we read through this book, are we passing God tests? We have forgotten who we are and about who made us. God have made us according to his plan, not according to anyone else plan. Think about it, if we go by God plan, we will not have to walk over anyone, if we follow God plan and start moving by God instruction we will pass. But remember in God eyesight we are great! Always remember it's all about God. Look everyone in this world has to answer to someone; why not let it be God? There is no one that can promise us that the sun will come up but God. It will be nice for a change to deal with a sure deal. God will help us to pass his tests, but remember it's up to us read below and understand.}

THE THREE STROMS

1. {We will be going into a storm- Mean the price of not following God plan; will determine how we will go in our storm. When we disobey God; he will sent us in a storm. Are we going into our storm today? Think about it!

2. Are we will be in a storm- Meaning everything is going wrong in our life, everything we try to do go wrong. Nothing seems to go right. Remember we must start to follow God plan in our heart. We must show God that we have remorse in our heart. We need to obey God in our heart. Then God will truth us again.

3. Are we will be coming out of a storm-When we start to following God plan in our heart, then God will let us come out of our storm. But always remember who brought you out of the

storm. Always learn from your storm. Sometime God bring us out of a storm and put us right back in a storm; are we passing any of our storms?

THESE TESTS WE WILL BE TAKING ALL OUR LIFE, ARE WE KEEPING IN MIND ANYTHING WE ARE LEARNING? AS WE GO THROUGH OUR STORM; ARE WE FOLLOWING GOD PLAN? OUR MONEY, OUR JOB, EVERYTHING WE CAN THINK OF BELONG TO GOD, WHAT DO WE THINK ABOUT THAT? CAN YOU THINK ARE ANYTHING THAT WAS NOT MADE BY GOD?}

GOD INTRODUCES PASTORS

God introduces pastors to the world in the Old Testament scripture and the New Testament: Just read and learn. "And I will give you pastors according to mine heart, which shall feed you with knowledge and understanding."Jer.3:15. {God know all of his pastors, before they were born, but we will not always wait on God, for he knows what we need at all time; are we faithfully following God instructions? Just look and understand this scripture below} "And I will set up one shepherd over them, and he shall feed them, even my servant David; he shall feed them, and he shall be their shepherd." Ezek.34:23. {The Bible is tells us things about God instruction? Please pay close attention to the following scriptures below we need the old and New Testament. The New Testament tells us what the words of Jesus teachers us.} "But Jesus said, forbid him not: for there is no man which shall do a miracle in my name that can lightly speak evil of me."Mar.9:39. And the New Testament tells us also that the words of Jesus teachers "And he gave some, apostles; and some, prophets; and some, evangelists; and some, pastors and teachers;" Eph.4:11. {Ok so tell me why then can't a woman preach His words. So my Bible also tells me that God use a rooster to remind a man who Jesus was. Just look at these scripture; *Being filled with all unrighteousness, fornication, wickedness, covetousness, maliciousness; full of envy, murder, debate, deceit, malignity; whisperers,*" "*Backbiters, haters of God, despiteful, proud, boasters, inventors of evil things, disobedient to parents,* "*Without understanding, covenant breakers, without natural affection, implacable, unmerciful:*" "*Who knowing the judgment of God, that they which commit such things are worthy of death, not only do the same, but have pleasure in them that do them.*" Rom.1:29-32. {Think about these Scriptures each one will cost us not to pass God tests. If we are doing them when we die we will go to hell. Remember heaven is a place for prepare people; if we not prepare we will not go to heaven but to hell.

THESE ARE THINGS THAT WILL HELP US

THESE THINGS WILL HELP US TO PASS GOD TESTS, JUST LOOK AND THINK AS WE READ BELOW TO UNDERSTAND:

- {Have family devotions daily; If not daily at lease two or three times a week. Remember God will be with you.
- Give God our best at all times. Remember you can lie to me but you can't lie to God. Think about it!
- Always give God the Glory for all things; not our self. But God will not keep blessing you if you don't.
- Live faithful at all time. Be faithful unto God all the days of your life.
- Remember it's all a test. But remember you do have a choice hell or heaven.}

REMEMBER GOD MADE IT ALL

{THINGS THAT WILL MAKE US FAIL GOD TEST OF FAITH, THINK ABOUT THESE TWO EXAMPLES}

- {"For the love of money is the root of all evil:"**1Tim.6:10a.** {We must pass God tests of faith in him before we die, have more righteous things in our life. Remember the soul can be saved, but the flesh cannot be saved.}
- "For all that is in the world, the lust of the flesh, and the lust of the eyes, and the pride of life is not of the Father, but is of the world." **1Joh.2:16.** {We will not pass as long as we hold on to things of this world; remember we have to deny ourselves to pass God tests, are we?}

A LOOK AT OUR PRAISE; LOOK AND LISTEN

REMEMBER OUR PRAISE IS MUCH MORE THEN A BODY ACTING, LOOK BELOW TO SEE. WHAT DO WE THINK? ARE WE PASSING GOD TESTS OF PRAISEING TO HIM TODAY LISTEN AND THINK?

{First-What if we were born without a voice; you mean we couldn't praise God? The highest praise is to obey God; this is the highest praising giving by man to God.}

Second-What if we were born without any hands? You mean we couldn't praise God? The highest praise is to obey God; this is the highest praise giving to man to obey God.}

Third-What if we were born without any legs? You mean we couldn't praise God? The highest praise is to obey God; this is the highest praise giving by God; to be obedient to him.}

{Yes we can give God the highest praise by obeying Him, in all things, following his Commandments and being faithful to Him. Remember these three things will get us into heaven, are we following God plan in glorify Him? Are we trying to glorify our self; think about it?}

THINK GOD BY PRAYING AND LISTEN

{ARE WE PASSING GOD TESTS OF FAITH? IF NOT, THEN PRAY TO JESUS. I REALIZE I'M A SINNER. FORGIVE ME FOR MY SINS, AND COME INTO MY HEART AND GIVE ME ETERNAL LIFE, AMEN. IF WE JUST BELIEVE IN OUR HEART AND HAVE FAITH IN GOD AND FOLLOW HIS PLAN AND NOT OUR PLAN WE WILL GO TO HEAVEN. WE NEED TO DO THIS, LISTEN! GOD HAS A PLAN OF SALVATION FOR US. ARE WE FOLLOWING GOD PLANS?}

If we are not going by God plan, repent now for our sins. Jesus has giving us a choice heaven or hell it's up to us. Do we have faith in God at all time? Think about it before we answer. Are we passing with our mouth or with our heart? Will we be ready when Jesus comes? He will not wait on us to get right. Look we will know that we are saved, if we are following God instruction. Remember we always can ask God to forgive us with our mouth, but what about our heart? Our heart is telling God we are just lying. Do we have the faith that God needs us to have in Him? Read the following scriptures to help us to understand.} "He that believeth on the Son of God hath the witness in himself: he that believeth not God hath made him a liar; because he believeth not the record that God gave of his Son." "And this is the record That God hath given to us eternal life, and this life is in his Son." "He that hath the Son hath life; and he that hath not the Son of God hath not life."1Jn.5:10-12. {Remember we are a stranger in a strange world living only by God Grace, are we following God plan? Jesus loves us so much he gave his life for us; can we believe someone loves us just that much? Think about it. Are we passing his test of faith? Have we forgotten that Jesus die for us? Know we turn away from God to man, are we passing God tests? Just look at what Jesus did for us.} "But he was wounded for our transgressions, he was bruised for our iniquities: the chastisement of our peace was upon him; and with his stripes we are healed".Isa.53:5. {Are we truly following God plan? There is no other plan that can save our soul but God plan. Look as the following scripture it will help us to understand.} "Neither is there salvation in any other: for there is none other name under heaven given among men, whereby we must be saved." Acts.4:12. {But remember Jesus Christ is salvation and his appeared on earth was to save us, he paid the price and became a living sacrifice for our sin, on the cross for us just think about it. In your life time what have you sacrifice for God? Remember God know when we or lying to Him. This scripture below will help us to understand.} "For then must he often have suffered since the foundation of the world: but now once in the end of the world hath he appeared to put away sin by the sacrifice of himself?" Heb.9:26. {Remember Jesus die for all that want to be saved, but remember Satan had his crew. There are some that don't want to be saved, so ever one didn't get saved. We much have a desire to be saved, by the only one that is able to saved, our creator. Think about it! Please don't be too late; when we of dead it will be too late. The expression in the Bible once saved always saved is true, but are we first saved are we just speaking from our mouth, are we save from the heart? Think about it, are we?}

ASK JESUS DAILY TO INTERCEDE FOR US

We must ask Jesus on a daily basic to intercede for us to pass God tests. "Wherefore he is able also to save them to the uttermost's that come unto God by him, seeing he ever lived to make intercession for them."Heb.7:25. {What do we think about that? Are we interceding for anyone or not? God will know if we are lying, everything we have read up to now we have seemed is before. Think about it, are we passing God tests? Seek ye the Lord while he may be found, call upon him while he can be found. Seek ye the Lord while he is near, for he will not be there for us always. Don't wait until we are dying. The wicked must say to God, forgive them for their sins. Forsake things are this world for him. The unrighteous man shall cry, for God mercy to be with them in death. Are we following God, or will this be us? Think about this.} "For as the heavens are higher than the earth, so are my ways higher than your ways, and my thoughts than your thoughts." Isa.55:9. {We must listen to the Lord to pass? Remember we will not live for ever, get right now. Will we be ready when the Lord comes? We need to get ready to meet God. We are getting closed and closed to death. Remember he is coming back for us maybe tomorrow, will we be ready? Remember it's easy to lie to our self. Listen do we not understand we will die and go to hell or to heaven? It's our choice, remembers Isa.55:9. But always remember we live only once in this world, but we much get ready too leave this world. But always remember heaven is a place for prepare people; heaven is not a place for every one think about it! are we prepare today? Remember the body will not go to heaven or hell, the body will return back to the ground, and the soul return back to God or go to hell. But remember your bodies mean nothing to God when you are dead, so remember this earth is passing away are we ready to meet God?}

HOW TO ENTER OUR FATHER KINGDOM

{We should know how to enter our father kingdom; the following scripture will help.} "Repent you therefore, and be converted, that your sins may be blotted out, when the times of refreshing shall come from the presence of the Lord;" Act.3:19. {Do we present our self to be a living sacrifice for the Lord at anytime, remember the way we live is the way we will die, but remember our life will tell on us to God. Remember someday we will get old, we can't tell who hands we will fall in before we die; always remember God have a plan. God know our heart; everything we do or say, it's all a test from God; are we passing today; think well about it before you answer?}

BAPTISMS WILL NOT SAVE US

{Look there is four baptisms spoken of in the New Testament. The first is the new birth, and we must be born again. Only the words of the Lord can save us not the water. We should know that being baptized will not save us. We much be saturated in the words of God into the Holy Spirit and the body of Christ. But second remember the water is symbiotic we go down in the water a dry Devil, and come up out of the water a wet Devil. Third there is water baptism, which is an outward sign of an inward grace. Four we much recognize and understand what we just read by doing this, Going to a good church that have a good Bible base Sunday school, and a good Bible study church, to become regenerated and renewed as a new creation in Christ. Those come through the words of Jesus from God. Which we can be save, if we believer the words of Jesus we can be save. Are we passing God tests today? Who did Jesus baptized or did he just saturated us in the words are His Heavenly Father through His teaching?} "Know you not, that so many of us as were baptized into Jesus Christ were baptized into his death?" "Therefore we are buried with him by baptism into death: that life as Christ was raised up from the dead by the glory of the Father, even so we also should walk in newness of life." "For if we have been planted together in the likeness of his death, we shall be also in the likeness of his resurrection: "Knowing this, that our old man is crucified with him, that the body of sin might be destroyed, that henceforth we should not serve sin" Rom.6:3-6. {Remember we must make a change from old to new and it starts slowly in our heart, giving up thing of this world and become Christ like. But we will not follow God plans. Remember we will not become a

Christian over night. Remember someone had to take time with us, think about it. If we are not having good days and bad days, up and down days we are not passing God tests. Ask your self can the Lord counts on us right know? Remember God didn't say we would have all good days; it's a gift from God, are we the one that count it all joy day by day? God is keeping his promises to us. Think about it; do we really understand who God really is? The words of God can save us, but remember there is not a sinless person in the world, but remember God is not a game that we can turn on or off when it convenient for us.

JUST A REMINDER

We should know that the church is just a stop off on our way home, think about it as a dressing room. Do we go to church just to be with other people, to catch up on the latest gossip, or see who we can talk about next week? But are we following God plan for us? Think about this; heaven or hell for our home. Jesus dies so we can make the right choice. Remember hell is not a weekend getaway it's for eternity, do we not understand? Hell is not a place to party, look we will not see our family there, and you will not see your friends there. Just look hell is a small room, where we will be in tormented days and nights we will not see light down that. Look at what it being says, we must recognize and understand that our body will return back to the ground from which we can. But remember it not your body that will speak for us, but the small vapor in our heart which is call your soul. Remember the Bible can't lie; we will not see our love one again after death. The Bible say flesh and blood shall not enter into heaven so think?

BELIEVE IT OR NOT IT'S ONLY A TEST

Long time before anything there was God. Even before time existed hours, minute, or seconds there was God. He created the universe, and before anything existed there was God! Between verses one and verse two of chapter one of Genesis there was a long span of time. But remember the Bible can't lie just listen. "In the beginning God, created the heaven and earth"Gen.1:1. {Look at in the beginning was God, and all things belong to God. God created the universes. God, Jesus, and the Holy Ghost are one spirit. But listen to what Jesus is saying?} "I and my Father are one." John 10:30. Remember Jesus can't lie; as we read this book along with our Bible think about what is being said. Listen to what the bible is saying; what do you think or we passing God tests? Remember no one knows but you and God if you are passing.} "And, Thou, Lord, in the beginning hast laid the foundation of the earth; and the heavens are the works of thine hands:"Heb.1:10. {God just say it and it happened; can you just magic in your mind how powerful

God is! But just remember he is God. Let's look at the bible scriptures to help us?} "Through faith we understand that the worlds were framed by the word of God, so that things which are seen were not made of things which do appear."Heb.11:3. {But understand that God did it all himself, know do we understand what God it saying? Please remember that God did is all for his pleasure, not our pleasure. Remember it's not about us, it's all about God.} "Who hath prevented me that I should repay him? Whatsoever is under the whole heaven is mine." Job.41:11. {Think about it; everything under the whole heaven is not our} "Even every one that is called by my name: for I have created him for my glory, I have formed him; yea, I have made him."Isa.43:7. {We can't stress this enough it's not about us, it's all about God. God is the creation of the universe. He made all the material for all things that was made. Read the following scripture to help you understand} "For thus saith the Lord that created the heavens; God himself that formed the earth and made it; he hath established it, he created it not in vain, and he formed it to be inhabited: I am the Lord; and there is none else." Is.45:18. {Read the following scriptures and pay close attention to all three} "In the beginning was the Word, and the Word was with God, and the Word was God." {His name is Jesus the son of God which is God.} "The same was in the beginning with God." {His name is Jesus the son of God which is God} "All things were made by him; and without him was not any thing made that was made."John.1:1-3. {God made all things with a word COME, do we ready believe that he created these things long before Adam. God has always been God, and he will always be God. Read the following scriptures for confirmation} "For this they willingly are ignorant of, that by the word of God the heavens were of old, and the earth standing out of the water and in the water:"2Pet.3:5. {From the beginning Jesus existed, the son of God which is Jesus, listen to God words as he talks to Job} "Where were thou when I laid the foundations of the earth? Declare, if thou hast understanding." "Who hath laid the measures thereof, if thou know? Or who hath stretched the line upon it?" "Whereupon are the foundations thereof fastened? Or who laid the corner stone thereof;" Job.38:4-6. {Some people say Job is just a myth, but where were you when God did it all? You can't answer because you didn't exist. God did himself, remember he own everything. God need no one helps to do anything. God did it all himself just listen to God words to understands?} "Who lay the foundations of the earth, that it should not be removed for ever."Ps.104:5. {Check out this scripture to help us understand, it's important that we understand?} "But, beloved, be not ignorant of this one thing, that one day is with the Lord as a thousand years, and a thousand years as one day." 2Pet.3:8. {Time is running out on us, will we pass? Are we ready for him? Are we passing God tests?} "But the day of the Lord will come as a thief in the night; in which the heavens shall pass away with a great noise, and the elements shall melt with fervent heat, the earth also and the works that are therein shall be burned up." 2Pet.3:10. {Are we following God plan? Are we passing most of God tests? Think about it hard before we answer, God see what ever our eyes see, God hear what ever we ears hear so we can't fool God.

God is everlasting higher then the world, and remember God is everlasting wider then the world. We can't go around God he is so bigger then the world, he is so low we can't go under, he is all we can think about and much more. Look God made angles in the image of Him to reign over his world. But one failed God by the name of Lucifer's, he was God beautiful angle and it went to his head. Lucifer was God angle of music but he let is all went to his head. Lucifer fails God test long before Adam, but look at this scripture is will help us, to understand what God is saying?} "Thou shalt not bow down thyself to them, nor serve them: for I the LORD thy God am a jealous God, visiting the iniquity of the fathers upon the children unto the third and fourth generation of them that hate me;" Ex.20:5. {Are we following God plan? thinking about it, as we read this book. Sometime we can put our foot in our mouth. Are we like Lucifer? Some of us think we are more than God, sometime we speak without thinking? Are we truly passing God tests, we can go to heaven or hell it's our choice? Lucifer was given a choice, he didn't pass. The name Lucifer appears only once in the bible, but he has many name that we will find thought out the bible, let's take a look and see now Lucifer fell from God grace. Look and listen.} "How art thou fallen from heaven, O Lucifer, son of the morning? How art thou cut down to the ground, which didst weaken the nations?"Is.14:12 {Look what God will do if we don't follow His instruction and listen to Him; remember the bible is his instruction book} "For thou hast said in thine heart, I will ascend into heaven, I will exalt my throne above the stars of God: I will sit also upon the mount of the congregation, in the sides of the north:"Is.14:12 {be careful what we think, do or react on it will cost us. God hear our heart and our thoughts, so we can't get over on God at any time; think about it. We can't lie to God but we think we can. Are we passing His test?} "I will ascend above the heights of the clouds; I will be like the most High." Isa.14:14. {That has weakened everything that is on the earth, we can say the wrong things sometime without thinking and it can cost us? God will test us all in our life times; will you pass? God tested Lucifer's with a little power, to reign over the earth, but he wanted more. Lucifer's rebellion again God and he fail his test. Remember God is testing us today? Are we failing God with a little power? God have given us a little authority over someone is we passing? When he gives us a little authority over something to test us, will we pass? God have giving us a great responsibility to watch over his body are we passing? Are we raise his children right according to the word, just listen to these scriptures as we think} "And I saw an angel come down from heaven, having the key of the bottomless pit and a great chain in his hand." "And he laid hold on the dragon, that old serpent, which is the Devil, and Satan, and bound him a thousand years," "And cast him into the bottomless pit, and shut him up, and set a seal upon him, that he should deceive the nations no more, till the thousand years should be fulfilled: and after that he must be loosed a little season." Rev.20:1-3. {What do you think about this? Is he in his season, what do you think? He is the falling angel who is the supreme enemy of God and all humankind. Are we trying to sell God out for anything that look and sound good to us? This world already belongs to God think about it. Just listen to this scripture.} "Thine heart was lifted up because of thy beauty; thou hast corrupted thy wisdom by reason of thy brightness: I will cast thee to the ground, I will lay thee before kings, that they may behold thee." Eze.28:17. {Because of Lucifer's there was a flood before the flood of Noah, but just listen to these scriptures and reflect back to your bible for more confirmation, but remember this is not of me, but of God} "I beheld the earth, and, lo, it was without form, and void; and the heavens, and they had no light." "I beheld the mountains, and, lo, they trembled, and all the hills moved lightly." "I beheld, and, lo, there was no man, and all the birds of the heavens were fled." "I beheld, and, lo, the fruitful place was a wilderness, and all the cities thereof were broken down at the presence of the Lord, and by his fierce anger." Jer.4:23-26. {But remember all this was by God in the beginning was God, all things were made by him; and without him were not any thing made and the beginning, and all this happen in Genesis one and one. But remember there was no light on earth, until judgment had been complete because of the sin of Lucifer.} "And the earth was without form, and void; and darkness was upon the face of the deep. And the Spirit of God moved upon the face of the waters." Gen.1:2. {When God started over again he will call back all thing that obey him, from the very beginning, just look at these scriptures below and think of what being said} "The thing that hath been, it is that which shall be; and that which is done is that which shall be done: and that is no new thing under the sun. "Ecc.1:9" One generation passeth away, and another generation cometh: but the earth abideth for ever." Ecc.1:4. {But always remember the devil is not after the father and the mother anymore he already have them, he is after our young generation think about it. Do we take up time with our children or do we take our children to church? If we have anything it's because God have given it to us. Do we ever pray with our children? Think about it. If we don't have the time for our children the devil does have the time. Look the devil have time to do what ever our children want. When our child or children need us to teach them about God will we know anything to teach them? What will you be able to tell them? Time is not on our side, we need to learn all we can and teach our children. We not only need to go to Sunday school, church and bible class, our children need to go. We need too study at home and church. We have no more time to get it right for our self are our children generation, so we need to remember that the devil is always asking God to let him test us twenty four hours a day. But just look at what God have already doing, God is forever the beginning and He will be the end. Are we passing God tests? Lucifer's was given a test in Genesis chapter one verses one and two: he didn't pass, and he didn't follow God plan. God destroy and erase all he had made. Everything that was on earth was underwater. God call back the water, after a longtime. Many years after the flood of Lucifer God started to restore habitation back to earth for a second time. But if we don't obey him he will destroy our generation: If we don't follow his plan and stop lying to ourselves and Him. If we are not following God plan for us remember what goes around will come around, this is your promise from God. So think about that before we react sometime. God will destroy us, if we don't follow his plan. Because He will end all life and will start over again! Think about it. God will start over again with all new creation. God is so good to His creation; He gives us a bible to help us step by step. But he will not make us used it. It's all a test. Did we learn anything from the first destruction of the world?} "For this they willingly are ignorant of, that by the word of God the heavens were of old, and the earth standing out of the water and in the water:" Whereby the world that then was, being overflowed with water, perished:" "But, beloved, be not ignorant of this one thing, that one day is with the Lord as a thousand years, and a thousand years as one day." 2Pet.3:5.6.8. {Thank about this; we have not made a minute in the sight of the Lord. We must make best out of our few minutes.

THE LORD IS CALLING BACK ALL RIGHTOUS THINGS

{The Lord is calling the earth back again from under the water. But remember because of the sins of Lucifer, he was bound for a thousand years, but he is loose and will deceive us. Remember God has not failed us one time. God is calling back everything that obeys Him and the light is again restored to the earth. God called the light out of darkness with one word "COME". God is the only one that can do that, not man. Man can supply us with light for a fee. God is so much more then the mind can imagine, what do you think?} And God called the light day and the darkness He calling night, and the evening and the morning were the first day. "Gen.1:1" The Lord made a firmament in the midst of the water, and he divided the water from the water. The firmament was made by God and he divided the water from the waters which were above, And God called the firmament heaven. And the evening and the morning were the second day. "Gen.1:8" {God let the water under the heaven be gathered together in one place, God say let the dry land appear: and it was so the dry land he called earth and the water he called Seas as it was told in Genesis chapter one verse nine. Listen God said let the earth bring forth grass, and let herb yield seed, and fruit tree yielding fruit after His own kind: and God saw that it was good and the morning were the third day. The lord lights the firmament of the heaven, to divide the day from the night, four seasons, and years. God was the light he said let it be light in firmament of the heaven, to give light upon the earth, do you understand? God made a great light to rule over day, and a less light to rule over the night: he also made the stars and the evening and morning was the fourth day. God creature great whales and every living created in the waters, brought forth abundantly after kind, and every winged fowl and God blessed them after his kind. God blessed them and said be fruitful and multiply and fill the water in the seas, and let fowl multiply in the earth. The evening and the morning were the fifth day, and God said let the earth bring forth the living creature after his kind, cattle, creeping thing, and every beast after there kind. "God said, let us make man in our image, after our likeness: and let them have dominion over the fowl of the air, and over the cattle, and over all the earth, and over every creeping thing that creepeth upon his earth as it was told in Genesis chapter one. {Remember this was before day six so God is giving angels another chance. What God said; in His image and not the image of Adam. Read the following scripture to understand.} "God is a Spirit: and they that worship him must worship him in spirit and in truth." John.4:24. {God made all people in His image and when He is ready to reveal His plan, He would wrap them as men and women. He did all this before day six, what do you think about that? Remember we will see this again for example God wrap Cain wife for him, we will see this later. Spirits are still out there, they are called litter angels of God. God saw every thing that he had made, and behold, it was very good, and the evening and the morning were the sixth day." Gen.1:31. {Look at what God made in five days; do we believe we could make anything without God authorities? He created all things even made a male and female before day six, and he didn't discriminate at all.

STILL DAY SIX

{God is looking over all He has done, and sees his plan coming together; are we passing? Think about it; still day six. Remember that we will see this again later in the book. The bible say He did finish on day six, and day seven he rested from all His work. The Lord said on day seven keep it holy; on to the Lord, for its the day of rest, we need to start to following God commandment at all time, because the Lord know when we of lying to Him. He knows the day we start to work; so from the first day count six days and rest on day seven. It's the Sabbath day to honor God, but remember God didn't say what day of the week it would be. It could be any day of the week Sunday, Monday, Tuesday, Wednesday, Thursday, Friday, or Saturday, are we passing today? Or are we on our way to hell? Are you following God one requests to rest on the seven day, are we passing today? God don't need our help for anything; all was made by God in six days. God just call the earth back from under the water, there was on rain. The bible did say the earth was cover under water, did it not say that? Think about that! The following passage will help us to understand. Can we just imagine seeing the world without any rain coming down from heaven, but it came out of the ground, or we passing? Just for the record the Lord had not caused it to rain upon the earth, but there when up a mist from the earth.} "And the Lord God formed man of dust of the ground and breathed into his nostrils the breath of life; and man became a living soul." Gen.2:7. {God form man out of the wet dust of the ground, He forms Him a man. Do we understand what this mean? We are no more than

- 18 -

dust, Remember God said He will not dwell in unclean places, so take a good look at the way we treat His body, because from the ground our body was taking so will it return back to the ground. Remember that God is lending us our body and someday the Lord will be back for it; will He find it in good condition? But remember all this was done before day seven. Adam was the first man God warped and shape and He molded around his soul, but remember the soul can't die but the body can, are we passing? Look! Its only day six think about it. God is giving man another responsibility besides the first one He gave to Lucifer, God trying again by giving man his first home in the Garden of Eden.

Remember it's all a test for man; Will he pass this time? Study your bible for a better understanding. Man first home on earth (the first one God ever formed) was on day six. But always remember at all time this is always just a test; will man pass? Are you passing today? Think about its! Still day six!.} "And out of the ground made the Lord God to grow every tree that is pleasant to the sight, and good for food; the tree of life also in the midst of the garden, and the tree of knowledge of good and evil"Gen.2:9. {And God is testing man at all times will we pass or not, what do you think? It's hard not to do something when someone tells us not to do it. Are we like that? Think about it before we answer. Remember God created a watering system to water the Garden of Eden. He made four rivers that running out of the Garden of Eden, to water the outside of the Garden. In Genesis chapter two verse ten through fourteen the rivers is name Psion, Gihon, Hidddekel, and the Euphrates, are we passing do we understand please read your bible for more information.} "And the Lord God took he man, and put him into the Garden of Eden to dress it and to keep it." Gen 2:15. {God have supply every thing for man; will we following his plan for us? What do we think; are we passing today? Remember we are still in day six; but look!} "And the Lord God commanded the man, saying, of every tree of the garden thou Mayes freely eat:" Gen. 2:16. {Listen to God as he gave man one commandment the Lord will not lie; one commandment was giving to man not to eat, off the tree of knowledge, of good and evil, are you will surely die. Remember this wills happing again just keep reading this book and remember, and we will understand?} "And the Lord God said it's not good that the man should be alone; I will make him and help meet for him." Gen.2:18. {God is always thinking about us, but man will face his greatest test. Adam was giving a great responsible, the authority to names all God creation; can He count on us for anything today, Are we worthy of God trust today? Are we truly following God plans for us today? Think about it! Look at God goodness He is always thinking of us, but we always taking advantage of God love. Are you today? God love man so He looks out for us at all times, are we passing God tests? But just look good as God give man his greatest gift, But look man will face his great test, will we pass are not?

A SURPRISE GIFT FOR MAN FROM GOD

"And the Lord God caused a deep sleep to fall upon Adam, and he slept: and he took one of his ribs, and closed up the flesh instead thereof;" Gen.2:21. {God perform the first surgery in the Garden of Eden. He uses no anesthesia and no tools. God perform the first transplant on man to make woman. He removed one of his ribs, and look! He closed it up, using no tools and made a woman. Please tell me you understand; God does not need man help with anything. Are you passing yet and what do you think about it? God brought Adam a great gift from his rib.} "And Adam said, this is now bone of my bones, and flesh of my flesh: she shall be called woman, because she taken out of man."Gen.2:23. {Man was giving the right to call woman anything and he calls her woman, because she was taking out of man. God made a woman using a rib from man that was made of dust of the ground, out side of the Garden of Eden. God made a woman; the first woman in side of the Garden of Eden, God performed the first marriage all in day six of creation. "Neither was the man created for the woman; but the woman for the man."1Cor.11:9. {Read the following scripture it will help you to pass God test today} "The thing that hath been, it is that which shall be; and that which is done is that which shall be done: and there is no new thing under the sun." "Is there any thing whereof it may be said, See, this is new? It hath been already of old time, which was before us." Ecc.1:9-10. {Everything we call new is not new to God, so remember we can try to find something new, but nothing of God is new is just recycle.

THE FIRST MARRIAGE

The institution of marriage was first performed by God, with Adam and Eve in the Garden of Eden. Are you following God plan? Refer to your bible and reminisce how good thing could be if we only follower God instruction; Are you following? But think about it! Are we truly passing any of God tests of love and compassion today? Would we be ready if God came today? Look at what is required of man; just one commandment to be faith to God. Remember man is in his greatest test now.} "Therefore shall a man leave his father and his mother, and cleave unto his wife: and they shall be one flesh."Gen.2:24. {Listen when a man takes on the responsibility of a wife, or a child or both, he leaves his father and mother, and become the head of his on family. He shall become a man when he leaves his father, and establish his on family with support and care. Are you a man today? It's easy to say I'm a father; but are we?}

FINALLY! DAY SEVEN AND THE DEVIL

"Thus the heavens and the earth were finished, and all the host of them. And on the seventh day God ended his work which he had made; and he rested on the seventh day from all his work which he had made. And God blessed the seventh day, and sanctified it: because that in it he had rested from all his work which God created and made." Gen.2:1-3. {As soon as God rested on day seven look what happen man sinned, God can't leave man along for a second; think about it. The devil reappears as a serpent to test man though the woman, remember it's all a test. It's just a test of our weakness in our faith with God; are we like that today? Think about it as we read below. The serpent devil move upon the face of the earth again to face the woman; he was looking for a weak point. God made the devil to be a test of our faith in him. Be careful what we say sometime the devil is always looking for a weak point in our life. We can't outsmart the devil without being obedient to God. We need to follow God instruction because the devil will try us twenty-four hours a day; are we passing today? Think about it! We must learn to follow all of God commandments by obeying Him. But the devil found a weakness in the woman.} "But of the fruit of the tree which is in the midst of the garden, God hath said, ye shall not eat of it, neither shall ye touch it, lest ye die." Gen.3:3. {But God told the man not to eat off the tree of knowledge or good and evil, God he didn't say nothing to the woman about touching or eat off the tree. The devil asked the woman what did God say and in return the woman said that God told us not to touch the tree of knowledge or the tree of good and evil. The devil said oh! I have her now the Lord didn't say anything to her about the tree. The serpent found a weakness in the woman she 'lying' on God. God didn't tell her anything; He told it only to the man. The serpents set her up to sin will; she passed are not? Are we passing? Think about it good before we answer. God was looking out for us before we were created; but we will not do the right things. Remember it's all about God; the tests are about your faith for Him. Remember God will let the devil test you anywhere, any day, are anytime, will you be ready? Remember God can't use us if He can't trusted us with anything; are we passing His tests? Think about it, are we just lying to ourselves and God? You have a choice heaven or hell. The woman is failing and so is the man, But the man was given the commandment from God, not to eat off the tree of knowledge or good and evil. But God didn't command the woman not to eat of the tree, but God did tell the man and look at man failing God test.} "And when the woman saw that the tree was good for food, and that it was pleasant to the eyes, and a tree to desire to make one wise, she took of the fruit thereof, and did eat, and gave also unto her husband with her; and he did eat."Gen.3:6. {God did not tell the woman she could not eat of the tree so she did eat, nothing happing when she ate of the tree. God didn't tell the woman the tree wasn't good for food, but He did say to the man don't eat. Look what happing when the man disobeyed God and ate of the tree, look remember Eve did not go and find her husband Adam, he was right there with her all the time as she eat of the tree. The bible didn't say He total the women not to eat. Look at Adam he didn't follow God commandment and he disobey God. Look today are we disobey God? Are we doing things against God will today? Lusting after things that do not belong to us.} "The eyes of them both were opened, and they knew that they were naked: and they sewed fig leaves together, and made themselves aprons."Gen.3:7. {Didn't anything happen still the man ate of the fruit from the tree, the Lord for bid him not to eat off the tree but when man ate all hell broke loose. Look what happing when the man disobey God, and they both seeing that they was naked and was ashamed. When the Lord tells us not to do something and we do it anyway it will cost us sometimes, think about it. Think before we act upon things sometime; ask yourself is this one of God tests for me? Be careful what we eat just because it looks good it just may not be good for us. The Lord tells us what is unclean and clean it's not good to eat ever thing. Just because it looks good it just may not be good for us, all things have a purpose; so are we passing today? Read these examples scriptures and see if we are passing God tests today} "And every beast that parted the hoof, and cleave the cleft into two claws, and cheweth the cud among the beasts, that ye shall eat." "Nevertheless these ye shall not eat of them that chew the cud, or of them that divide the cloven hoof; as the camel, and the hare, and the Coney: for they chew the cud, but divide not the hoof; therefore they are unclean unto you." "And the swine, because it divides the hoof, yet cheweth not the cud, it is unclean unto you: ye shall not eat of their flesh, nor touch their dead carcass." "These ye shall eat of all that are in the waters: all that have fins and scales shall ye eat:" "and whatsoever hath not fins and scales you may not eat; it is unclean unto you." Deu.14:6-10. {Remember it's why we are so sickly today, because we will eat anything that look good to us, but remember it's your choice to live on this earth health of not, but remember God say the body it a temper to keep holy only into God look are we think about it?} "And they heard the voice of the LORD God walking in the garden in the cool of the day: and Adam and his wife hid themselves from the presence of the LORD God amongst the trees of the garden."Gen.3:8. {Sometime it's good to wait and cool off before taking action, look parents are we setting a good example for our children? Look remembers we will always be God children, are we disappointing God and disobey His commandment. We need to look at children action today just to understand. We are acting like our children when it comes to God. Remember when the woman ate off the tree didn't anything happens; because the Lord didn't commandment the woman not to eat but to the man. Are we following God instructions today are we passing God tests today?}

Remember God see us when no one else can.

WILL WE BLAME SOMEONE
ELSE FOR OUR ACTION?

"And he said I heard thy voice in the garden, and I was afraid, because I was naked; and I hid myself."Gen.3:10. {Sin will call us out and make us see the nakedness of our body. We must follow God instruction today; are we naked?} "And he said, who told thee that thou wast naked? Hast thou eaten of the tree, whereof I commanded thee that thou shouldest not eat?" Gen.3:11. {But the man trying to blame the woman; are we trying to blame someone else for our sins? Just think! We can't lie to God, are you? But God didn't tell the woman; He told the man not to eat of the tree. Listen to God as He says to Adam who did I leave in charge the woman or you? Think about it before you respond. We are always looking for a fall guy; we must learn to expect our on responsibility for our action. Are we following God instructions? Are we passing God tests?} "And the Lord God said unto the woman, what is this that thou hast done? And the woman said the serpent beguiled me, and I did eat." Gen.3:13. {The word beguiled means to deceive, but remember God didn't tell the woman not to eat. But the serpent deceive her and she did eat but always remember the serpent called the devil is on duty twenty-four hours a day, are we going to do what he say? We have a desire to sin; we much put on a full armor of God each day. Are you passing? Think about it! The following scripture below will help us.} "But I fear, lest by any means, as the serpent beguiled Eve through his subtilty, so your minds should be corrupted from the simplicity that is in Christ." 2Cor.11:3. {But this doesn't excuse Adam for his disobey God commandment but listen. God cursed the serpent by taking his legs away; remember the serpent used to walk up right but no more, he was cursed to crawl upon his stomach and to eat the dust for all the days of his life. "And I will put enmity between thee and the woman, and between thy seed and her seed; it shall bruise thy head, and thou shalt bruise his heel." Gen. 3:15 {God have all power over everything, but are we following God? He knows when we are lying? Read this scripture.} "He that committed sin is of the devil; for the devil sinned from the beginning. For this purpose the son of God was manifested, that he might destroy the works of the devil," 1John.3:8. "Unto the woman he said I will greatly multiply thy sorrow and thy conception; in sorrow thou shalt bring forth children; and thy desire shall be to thy husband, and he shall rule over thee."Gen.3:16. {Listing to what God is saying to the woman only her husband should she desire, if a woman is not marriage and in her own house then she is the head of her house, she will be care for by God. God will be her husband; men are we the head of our house? Think before we answers. But remember to be a family of God on this earth; we will need to be able to reproduce according to God. Some men are still a child in a man's body but a man need to be a man. Are we passing God tests today? Are we a true man today? Look at the scriptures below; remembers this will help you in life and to understand} "But I would have you know, that the head of every man is Christ, and the head of Christ is

God." 1Con.11:3. "And unto Adam He said, because thou hast hearkened unto the voice of thy wife, and hast eaten of the tree, of which I commanded thee, saying, thou shalt not eat of it: cursed is the ground for thy sake, in sorrow shalt thou eat of it all the days of thy life;" Gen.3; 17. {Adam was cursed for eaten the fruit that God had commanded him not to eat. And he cursed Adam for listen to his wife, and ate off the tree and which he was the overseer of in the garden, and by doing the one thing He told him not to do, Adam hide because he disobey God. Man has to work for all his food from the ground, man mess him self up, are we messing our self up over lusting for something? Are we following God instructions today? Are we truly passing his tests today? From dust we came and dust we will return. We have to till the ground until we return back to the ground, are we passing his tests today? Think about what your heavenly Father is saying, would we be ready if Jesus came today? Are we truly! Truly! Truly passing God tests? Remember it's not about us, our wealth or richest; remember our body will still go back to dust. If we are not doing the right thing our soul will not go to heaven, but our body will go back to the ground.} "All go unto one place; all are of the dust, and all turn to dust again." Eccl.3:20. {Remember we have no say so over where God body return back to. But a disobedient soul will go to hell. Obedient souls will be judges by God from there heart; our choice. Now we are being tested daily of our faith and our love for God. Are we passing His tests of love for Him today? The Lord was the only one that made skin without using animals to cover up humans in the Garden of Eden. Look even when we let God down He will takes care of us. But remember ask God daily to forgive us for our sins. If we die before we ask God to forgive us, He care enough to make sure we go to heaven or hell; think about it? Adam and Eve was expel from the garden because the tree of life was in the garden. Remember in the garden was another test that they wouldn't pass, what we do think? Man has already disappointed God. Are we disappointing God today? Think about this: have things start to happen in our life we can't explain? Maybe we are not following God plan? If we were in the Garden of Eden would we had passed that test? God didn't trust them anymore because they had failed.} "So he drove out the man; and He placed at east of the garden of Eden with Cherubims, and a flaming sword which turned every way, to keep the way of the tree of life."Gen.3:24. {The first eviction was doing by God to Adam and Eve; from the Garden of Eden do we understand? He seals the open from the human eye. Because the tree of life was in the garden they would take advantage of God. Man was now kicked out are the garden because he didn't follow God instruction. God made everything for man convenient, but because of man greediness he was kicked out of his first home and now man must live by this work of his own hands, because of his greediness he didn't pass God test of obedient. Just look what lying can cause us in life. The first birth generation of Adam's is an example of what not to do to pass God test. One thing to do to pass God tests is have faith in Him at all time in all things. Remember what going on around us it's all about a test. But God is always doing the best for us, it's only a test; will we follow God plan or our plan?}

CAIN AND ABEL

"And Adam knew Eve his wife and she conceived, and bare Cain, and said, I have gotten a man from the Lord."Gen.4:1 {Cain was the first child ever born in the world and was born out side of the garden. He was a cursed child through his father and mother sins.} "And she again bares his brother Abel. And Abel was a keeper of sheep, but Cain was a tiller of the ground."Gen.4:2. {Adel was the Second child born in the world, he was a keeper of sheep, and he loved God so very much. The first born like his father was a tiller of the ground. But the Lord want our very best at all time but Cain is failing God test, are we failing his test?} "And in process of time it came to pass, that Cain brought of the fruit of the ground an offering unto the Lord. Gen.4:3. {But Cain didn't bring God his best, he brought God his leftovers, God does not need our leftovers at any time, Give God our very best at all times. Are we like Cain today given God our leftovers, do we give God your best at all times, do we really think we can fool God at anytime? Look at the following scriptures, what do you think?} "All the best of the oil, and of the wheat, the first fruits of them which they shall offer unto the Lord, them have I given the." Num.18:12. {Adel is passing because he is giving God his best, Adel is an example of what should be done in life, are we given God our best? think about it as we read.} "And Abel, he also brought of the firstlings of his flock and of the fat thereof. And the Lord had respect unto Abel and to his offering:" Gen.4:4. {And the Lord respect Abel because he brought him his best, but Cain offering to God was rejected; that made Cain jealous of his brother. Abel loved God more then anything, but just think about this; has loving something so much you're willing to give up your life. Remember the following scripture for better understanding.} "By faith Abel offered unto God a more excellent sacrifice than Cain, by which he obtained witness that he was righteous, God testifying of his gifts: and by it he is being dead yet speaket."Heb.11:4. "But unto Cain and to his offering he had not respect. And Cain was very wroth, and his countenance fell." Gen.4:5. {God doesn't need our left over at anytime; give God our very best at all time, when your money is low gives God your best; are we passing? When bills are due; give God your best. When home need work, give God your best. When you don't have a job give God ten percent of what He blessed you with; think about it.} "And the Lord said unto Cain, Why art thou wroth? And why is thy countenance fallen?" Gen.4:6. {When we are a selfish person we will not be happy, we will always be jealous of things and some one, but we will not pass God test of faith. Always do thing to glorify God and not you're self. Are we following God plan for us? Are we trying to fool God? Think about it. God it no one fool. Cain is failing God test because he thinks God will take anything. Cain is the example of what we should not do.} "And Cain talked with Abel his brother: and it came to pass, when they were in the field, that Cain rose up against Abel his brother, and slew him." Gen.4:8. {The first murder in the world was done by Cain to his brother. Cain was jealous of his brother Abel, just think about this; brothers are we jealous of our brothers today? Remember always give God your very best at all time. But God didn't respect Cain offering because it was not his best. God was pleased with Abel offering because it was his best. And the Lord said unto Cain, where is Abel thy brother? Yes! Cain lies to God; he knows he is his brother keeper, are we our brother's keeper today? Think about it; are we following God plan for us today?} "And He said what hast thou done? The voice of thy brother's blood cried unto me from the ground."Gen.4:10. {Remember we can't lie to God. God will call us out when we sin, look at what happen when we take something we can't give back, have we done anything that cost us not to pass God test of faith? Think about it! But are we following God plan for us? This could be us? Remember we can't lie to God at any time about anything, He sees all our sins! We can't hide anything from Him; think about it. Are we passing God test? Just look! God cursed the ground not to grow anything unto Cain. Think about it as we read about Cain.} "And Cain said unto the Lord, My punishment is greater than I can bear."Gen.4:13. {Thank God he never put more on us then we can bear, so if we can't take God punishments then don't do the sin. If we receive God rules, and don't follow them we will be punished by God, Cain was the first to show remorse in the world. Have we being truly remorse at anytime in our life like Cain is now? Read this scripture as an example?} "And in hell he lifts up his eyes, being in torments, and seeth Abraham afar off, and Lazarus in his bosom." Luke16:23 {The Lord wills punish you for all your sins, remember God have a punishment for us great then death; just keep on sinning. God will punish us like the rich man. The Lord will be established his law for man. God will be introductions the Lord punishment outside of the Garden of Eden. When we disobey God; will we be failing his test?} "And the Lord said unto him, therefore whosoever slayeth Cain, vengeance shall be taken on him sevenfold. And the Lord set a mark upon Cain, lest any finding him should kill him." Gen.4:15. {Cain had to be very careful he had to learn from his mistake, because God had not established His law outside of the Garden of Eden. God created other people long before Adam like the wife of Cain God just wrap her: What do you think? Cain action cost him to be a fugitive and a vagabond.} "And Cain went out from the presence of the Lord, and dwelt in the land of Nod, on the east of Eden." Gen.4:16. {When we sin against God and take someone life it's a sin. Are we following God plan are we passing his tests today? Remember all we had heard; we will hear over and over again in this book. But look God will forgive us if we asked forgiveness in our heart, He will forgive us. But remember what we read we will see it again} "The thing that hath been, it is that which shall be; and that which is done is that which shall be done: and there is no new thing under the sun,"Ecc.1:9. {Do you understand? Just listen how good God is to us.} "And Cain knew his wife; and she conceived, and bare Enoch and he builder a city, and called the name of the city, after the name of his son, Enoch." Gen.4:17. {The Lord blessed Cain with a wife and she was one of many that God wrapped her spirit on day five. Cain first son became the third man born in the world; Cain built a city for his first born son in the world in the land of nod, and names the city after his son Enoch. This is the generations of Adam son through Cain look its right there in the Bible.} "And unto Enoch was born Irad begat Mehujael begat Methusael begat Lamech 'he took unto him two wives and was the first recorded man with two wives and there names was Adah and Zillah. Lamech did the second murder recorded in the world and was Cain grandson. His punishment was greater then Cain and our punishment will be greater today. We will go to hell for taking something we can't replace back. "And Adam lived an hundred and thirty years, and begat a son in his own likeness, after his image; and called his name Seth:" Gen.5:3. {The Lord blesses Adam with one more son, Are you follow God plan today? look Seth replace Adam son Abel; think about what is happing?} "And the days of Adam after he had begotten Seth were eight hundred years: and he begat sons and daughters: Gen.5:4. {Adam lives to get more sons and daughters after Seth. But! Seth would be the one that Noah was descending from, think about it? God bless his children; do you understand?} "And all the days that Adam lived were nine hundred and thirty years: and he died." Gen.5:5. {Adam lived one hundred and twelve years after the birth of Seth, his third son. Seth begins of a new generation of Adam grandchildren will they pass God tests?} "And Seth lived an hundred and five years, and begat Enos:" "And Seth lived after he begat Enos eight hundred and seven years, and begat sons and daughters:"Gen.5:6. {But listen} "And all the days of Seth were nine hundred and twelve years: and he died."Gen.5:7.8. {A new begin through the generations are Seth, Think about it as you look at the generation below?} "And Enos lived ninety years, and begat Cainan:" "And Enos lived after he begat Cainan eight hundred and fifteen years, and begat sons and daughter" "And all the days of Enos were nine hundred and five years: and he died." Gen.5:9.10.11.

THE GENERATIONS

{Look at the generation countdown, do you see God plan? Keep looking!} "And Cainan lived seventy years, and begat Mahalaleel:" "And Cainan lived after he begat Mahalaleel eight hundred and forty years, and begat sons and daughter:" "And all the days of Cainan were nine hundred and ten years: and he died."Gen.5:12.13.14. {Look at God plan coming together, Are you following God plan today? These are your descendants, just look!} "And Mahalaleel lived sixty and five years and begat Jared" "And Mahalaleel lived after he begat Jared eight hundred and thirty years, and begat sons and daughters:" "And all the days of Mahalaleel were eight hundred ninety and five years: and he died." Gen.5:15.16.17. {Remember all these generations had to take place good or bad, so God can see if He can count on us. Look at what God do next!} "And Jared lived an hundred sixty and two years, and he begat Enoch:" "And Jared lived after he begat Enoch eight hundred years, and begat sons and daughters:" "And all the days of Jared were nine hundred sixty and two years: and he died." Gen.5:18.19.20. "And Enoch lived sixty and five years, and begat Methuselah:" "And Enoch walked with God after he begat Methuselah three hundred years, and begat sons and daughters:" "And all the days of Enoch were three hundred sixty and five years:" "And Enoch walked with God: and he was not; for God took him." Gen.5:21.22.23.24. {Enoch was dedicated to God and God reward him, he was transported or taken directly into the present of God, without experiencing death. But always remember no book nowhere say he was transported into heaven, but that he walked with God; think about it!} Just look at the following these are the generations; "And Methuselah lived after he begat Lamech seven hundred eighty and two years, and begat sons and daughters:" "And all the days of Methuselah were nine hundred sixty and nine years: and he died." Gen.5:25.26.27. {Always remember Lamech was the father of Noah. Methuselah was the longs living man on earth that is record; he almost lived one day according to the Lord. The following scripture will help.} "But, beloved, be not ignorant of this one thing, that one day is with the Lord as a thousand years, and a thousand years as one day." 2Pet.3:8. {Now tell me what you think; look!} "And Lamech lived an hundred eighty and two years, and begat a son:" "And he called his name Noah, saying, this same shall comfort us concerning our work and toil of our hands, because of the ground which the Lord hath cursed." "And Lamech lived after he begat Noah five hundred ninety and five years, and begat sons and daughters:" "And all the days of Lamech were seven hundred seventy and seven years: and he died. And Noah was five hundred years old: and Noah begat Shem, Ham, and Japheth." Gen.5:28-32. {The Lord has come full circle from the generations of Cain and Abel and the second murder ever recorded. Remember down from Seth, God have been blessing down to Enoch. God walked with Enoch and Noah. Can He use you for anything today? Look at God through this generation. Now tell me what you think! And from the generation of Seth Lamech begat a son. And he called his name Noah, saying, he shall comfort us. But look at the Lord! He looks through the generations to see if we would obey Him today, are we following his instruction? God found favor in Noah; can He find favor in us today? Noah was five hundred years old: and Noah begat Shem, Ham, and Japheth. Remember down from Seth God have walked with, and blessing him down to Enoch, God walked with him down to Noah. God also walk with and blessed Noah. Are we following God plan? Can we walk by His plan today? God had become tried of man sinning all the time. Just listen as God talk to Noah when men begin to multiply on the face of earth. These giants start to take wives of there brothers, corruption was all around; they started to sin, drink and party all the time.} "And the Lord said, my spirit shall not always strive with man, or that he also is flesh: yet his days shall be an hundred and twenty years." Gen.6:3. {God is very up set with man;

it's time to get right know. God is always testing us. Take time and look at your life. Look the days of man sinning is running out, will we be ready for God when He coming back? Let's not wait to long. God is giving Noah a time of an hundred and twenty years to try to change man heart and mind from evil to good. Noah denied himself of all the worldly things. Remember our work and faith will be all we will have to speak for us. Are we doing the will of God and following his commandment? Noah had to first realize he is part of God plan. The second he realize the Lord will gives him the strength to convince his wife he is not crazy. She realizes everything Noah was doing is the will of God. His whole family realize what he was doing was the will of God; we much realize the will of God. Can we just imagine what he was gone through every day and night? Preachers, Pastors, Minister, and Evangelist have a sworn duty to God to preach the gospel; are we doing that today? Just remember God have a plan for us today. Can God count on us right now? Think about it, He will not wait for ever on us. Remember we all have to give up something for God; have we being given up anything?} "There were giants on the earth in those days; and also after that, when the sons of God came in unto the daughters of men, and they bare children to them, the same became mighty men which were of old, men of renown." Gen.6:4. {Think about it; are we sons and daughters of angels that have fallen from God's grace? Have you fallen from God grace today? Can God count on us to be leaders for Him? Children are we passing today? The sight of man was complete failing God like we are today. God is on his way back: will we be ready or not? It grieved God that He had made man. Man is losing God respect again because of there sinful way; God commands us time after time not to sin and all we do it sin. The Lord is not a game to play; He is the master of the universe. I will destroy man whom I have created from the face of the earth, because man disobeys me. The earth is filled with violence throughout; we don't know God, but He will destroying all life and start over again. Are we following God instructions today? Are we passing his tests? Like today we are disappointing God and not passing his tests, be truthful with your self. God knows when we are lying. God will not let our sin go unpunished, at anytime. God will destroy all He had creation and start over. Are we following God instructions today, listening to God as he gives Noah instructions.} "Make thee an ark of gopher wood; rooms shalt thou make in the ark, and shalt pitch it within and without with pitch."Gen.6:14. {Noah is Following the Lord instructions, are we following the Lord instruction today? are we capable are passing God tests today? Remember its God way; not our way.} "And this is the fashion which thou shall make it of: The length of the ark shall be three hundred cubits, the breadth of it fifty cubits, and the height of it thirty cubits. Gen.6:15. {Those instructions were from the Lord, are we following the right instruction today? God have a plans for us, but we always let him down, the Lord gave Noah instruction} "A window shalt thou make to the ark, and in a cubit shalt thou finish it above; and the door of the ark shalt thou set in the side thereof; with lower, second, and third stories shalt thou make it." Gen.6:16. {If we following God instruction we will not go wrong, are we following God instruction today, tell the truth are we listen to God? God is getting tried, He have give us enough time to get is right, but man is still lying and sinning. Are we being faithful to the Lord? Are we lying to our self think about it, God see our every moves. God told Noah all out side the ark will be destroyed, if they don't follow His commandment. Noah did all things according to the God instructions, are we today?

LOOK IS WE READY FOR GOD JUDGMENT

We never know when God is coming back; Think about it! If he came today would we pass His tests? Can the Lord count on us? Can God found any righteousness in us or our family? Remember only we can make the right choice; not our family. God gave Noah his instruction to follow; God have a plan and we much follow His plan. God is the only one that can save us. Are we making the right decision? God is the only one that can give us the right instructions, listen to God as he gives the instruction to Noah. God have a plan, do we understand? Think about it as we read below: God will never lie to us; are we ready for Him? Think about it. If we follow God instructing for us; we can have a long life. Are we following God instruction? The Lord wills always keep his promise to us, but we will not keep our promise to Him. He knows all our thoughts, all the things we do, things we do to other; He see. Are we passing? Remember it's only a test; don't wait until the last minute and try to follow God instruction. To replenish the earth of all his creating, He will not create them again} "There went in two and two unto Noah into the ark, the male and the female, as God had commanded Noah." Gen.7:9. {Noah did according to the Lord, are we following the Lord's command? It's the only test that we much pass in life? As we see the Lord doesn't lie, are we lying about our love for God today? Remember he is coming will we be ready? An a hundred and twenty years late, just as God promised, it began to rain the first rain, and the longest rain recorded. God always keep his promises. "And it came to pass after seven days that the waters of the flood were upon the earth." {As you see the Lord doesn't lie, are you lying about your love for God today, remember He is coming, will you be ready?} "In the six hundredth year of Noah's life, in the second month, the seventeenth day of the month, the same day were all the fountains of the great deep broken up, and the windows of heaven were opened."Gen.7:11. {An a hundred and twenty years late, just as God promised, it began to rain the first rain, and the longest rain recorded, and the world remembered, God always keep his promises, do you think you are listen? There is a song called "Open the Flood Gates of Heaven" and it say let it rain, we need to be careful what we ask God. He will sometime just give us what we ask, if you were outside the ark today: will you be ready for the rain? Think about it. God is always giving us time after time; just think about it. All at once the rain start to come down; what would you think. Keep in mind the door to the ark was lock; just imagine if that was us out side the ark. Can we just imagine how they felt after the water rose higher and higher. They realized there was no way into the ark, can we just imagine all the praying and all the lying to God that was being doing. God is a good God and He always keeps his promises. Will we be too late in life? We have been warned day after day, are we passing our tests from Him today? If not we will go to hell; if we are not right with God. Look at man disappointing God for there own lust and for there own gratification. Lucifer lusted for self gratification and power cause the first flood on earth. Man lusting after self gratification causes the second flood upon the earth; are we passing? Remember He knows when we are lying to Him. It's our choose heaven or hell it up to us: don't wait to long. He have given us our whole life time to get ready, will we be ready? He is coming soon, think about it. God will make good on His promise; He is coming again; will we be ready? A total are eight people follow God commandment, His instructions and obeying Him; think about it. Would we have been one of the eight? The Lord commanded Noah to put every thing of it kind on the ark; the Lord sent all of them to Noah while he builds the ark: are we following the Lord instruction? I will repeat just so we can understand. All God creation follows his commanded two by two. Enter the ark two by two included Noah family; are we following God plan today?} "And they that went in, went in male and female of all flesh, as God had commanded him: and the Lord shut him in." Gen.7:16. {One of each sex enter the ark; God have a plan for us to follow, are we following His plan? We must be doing things God way to replenish the earth. He didn't say two male they couldn't replenish the earth, He didn't say two female they couldn't replenish the earth. Remember this will be the second flood that comes upon the earth.} "And the flood was forty days upon the earth; and the waters increased, and barn up the ark, and it was lift up above the earth." Gen.7:17. {As the Lord had promised Noah it would happen, are you passing today think about it? God is coming don't let it be too late. And the waters prevailed out side the ark all over the face of the earth. Will we be ready? Are we following God instruction? Everything under heaven was destroyed except the ones on the ark. Just like today we have been warned, but are we taking God serious? Everything was covered under water except upon the ark. But look God do not lie He always keep him promise. All life that was off the ark was dead. God is good at all time; see how He is taking care of Noah and his family. The Lord made a wind to pass over the earth and remover the water from the earth. God stop the rain by speaking one word "stop", do we not believe he is coming again, think about it. Don't be the one that get caught in the rain; you being warned.} "And the waters returned from off the earth continually: and after the end of the hundred and fifty days the waters were abated."Gen.8:3. "{It was a lot of water on the earth; it took a long time to return back, are we prepared for our earth shattering storm? Remember its coming. God put a high mountain for the ark to rest upon; God is good at all times. See how long the water was on the earth, before God call it back. God have given us a long time to get ready, for His return. Can we just imagine all the dead bird and dead people on the top of the ark? How hard was it to opening up the window to the ark with all the skeleton laying on top of the window? Adam Generation was brought over through the flood on the ark. Noah opens the window and the sun can into the ark for the first time after the flood. Noah needs an animal to send out to check for land. He sent the wrong one out to check; he sends the raven for he wasn't going to do the job. The raven wasn't going to leave the food on the ark; he is not passing the test. He then waited seven days and then sent the right one, a dove. The dove will look for dry land; the dove will look good before he return back to them. Do you see God plan coming together? The dove couldn't find dry land to rest, so he returns back to the ark. Noah waited seven more days before he send the dove back, but remember that the Lord have a plan. He's teaching Noah how to be patience. God is teaching Noah and his family how to be patient; we must wait on God for His plan to work. Are you waiting on him today?} "And the dove came in to him in the evening; and, lo, in her mouth was an olive leaf pluck off: so Noah knew that the waters were abated from off the earth."Gen.8:11 "{Remember seven days is a completion for God work. So on day seven Noah sent the dove black out to looks for dry ground again by faith, are we doing thing by faith for God. Are or we doing thing our way or you passing God test today? Only God can do this; do we have faith in God? God said I have a plan yet for you and your family, are we following God plan today? Remember the Lord knows our heart; look at what God is saying.} "Go forth of the ark, thou, and thy wife, and thy sons, and thy sons' wives with thee." Gen.8:16. {These are the generations we came down from, starting from the great, great grandfather in which his name was Adam. The great grandfather name Seth, down to the grandfather in which his name is Lamech, down to the son in which his name was Noah. God found grace in which He brought us from old to the new generation and it all was a test. Will you have faith in God, and follow His instructions?} "And Noah went forth, and his sons, and his wife, and his sons' wives with him:" Gen.8:18. {Look at what God will do; He will destroy again with a flood, and He will start over again by saying one word "come", just like in the beginning of Genesis.1:1-2 think about it. Remember everything that came off the ark was made by God, are we passing God tests? Do we understand? What do we think about it today? For all things we must give thanks to the Lord, do we give thanks to God at anytime? Are we giving thanks to man instead of the Lord?} "And in the second month, on the seven and twentieth day of the month, was the earth dried."Gen.8:14. {Only God can do this do you have the faith in Him, are you passing God test today? think about it.} "And God spake unto Noah, saying,"Gen.8:15. {I have a plan yet for you and your family, are you following God plan today? Remember the Lord knows your heart look at what God is saying.} "Go forth of the ark, thou, and thy wife, and thy sons, and thy sons' wives with thee." Gen.8:16. {Remember it's all a test will you have faith in God, and follow all his instructions?} "Bring forth with thee every living thing that is with thee, of all flesh, both of fowl, and of cattle, and of every creeping thing that creepeth upon the earth; that they may breed abundantly in the earth, and be fruitful, and multiply upon the earth." Gen.8:17. {Saying I will not cause the ground any living thing again for man sins, do we think we are passing God tests today? Are we following God plan for us? But remember our time is running out, will we be ready when He comes? Remember He said He will be back, and He will not curse the ground for man sin. God have control over all living things; just look around and see. God work is all around us: think about it. The Lord blessed Noah and his sons to be fruitful, and to multiply. They had a great job to replenish the earth; can the Lord count on us for such a great job today? He didn't say what race but he said to be fruitful, and multiply, and replenish the earth, think about it. Two men can't do the job and neither can two women. God is given them a prestigious job; can God count on us like that today? Will we deny our self and follow God plan? Are we obeying God? Are we listening to God instruction today? God is once again putting His trust in man with a prestige job; will we pass this time? Can we handle this job? Just look at us today, can the Lord count on us? Remember God have a plan? Will we follow God plan? Think about it; are we passing God tests today? We much follow God instructions for He has a plan, which we all must go by to pass His test? Noah and His sons have a great job to do; but the question is will they obey all God instruction? Are you passing His test today? Look He will blessed them all for there obedience, are we being obedient to God? Are we being truthful to our self and God? Remember He trust us today, He is on his way back; will we be ready? God said he will not punish the earth for man sin no more, is we passing? Are we following God instructions He is come back one day soon; will we be save? God made a covenant with all that was on the ark for all generations; we are one of the future generations. Are we passing for our children? Think about it! He didn't say sin was ok, but He did say every one will be accountable for there on sins. God have a plan; will we be part of God plan or not? But He is saying if we die before we ask forgiving we will go to hell. This is a promise from God; are we living a lie? Think about it. Look at these scripture to remind us and help us make the right choice.} "I will make an everlasting covenant with them, that I will not turn away from them, to do them good; but I will put my fear in their hearts that they shall not depart from me." Jer.32:40. {These are God words, do not failures Him. He will send us to hell. He is God and He makes all of the rules don't try Him; He is not a game. I repeat He is not a game. If you are not right, get right please! But look; we will always mess up: we need to think sometime before we react. It's not ok to drink wine; that control our mind. It's not good to let anything control us but God; in order to pass his test. Noah was the first to fail under God new rules; because he drunk and lose control of his mind. The word wine is mention for the first time in the Old Testament. Remember there are two different wines; sometime it's good to reference to your bible or a bible dictionary. Stop lying to God and to your self for your gratification. Ham the youngest son violates his father by going to his tent without permission. Ham the second to fail under God new rulers; are we failing God new rules today? Do we not understand there are some things we just don't do. Think about it. People look! We know right from wrong, but we are not passing, we are failing. Listen! All of these little things we do in the dark we will be punishment for them, but always remember God are looking right at us. But Noah knows his two oldest sons wouldn't do something to him, but Ham is another story. Ham father cursed him to be a low servant of his brothers, can anybody counts on us today? Right now! Are you passing God tests today? Noah cursed Ham to be a servant to Shem his brothers, Ham was not trustworthy to be a man of authority, is we trustworthy to have God authority? {Both brothers live in one tent that means Ham was servant to both brothers, it's not good to do certain things that you know is wrong; it can cost you. "And Noah lived after the flood three hundred and fifty years." And all the days of Noah were nine hundred and fifty years: and he died. Gen."9:28.29. {The Lord was still good to Noah, maybe Noah asks God to forgive him before he died. The bible didn't say if Noah asks God forgiving; that is between God and Noah. Look how good God is: He is a forgiven God. If we ask God to forgiving us in our heart before we died and mean it; He will. He will forgive us, just try him and see. But we must say it from our heart not our mouth. Let not wait until we get sick, it will be to last. Noah was giving a test and he follows all commandments; so please understand it's easy to get right with God. Just look at these following scriptures, they will help us. If we follow God commandment in our heart just try him and see just try him for your self. What do we think our choice will be? Heaven or hell! thinks about it. Please be careful before you answer. We have learned no one is perfect on this earth but look. God is giving man another tests will we pass?} "And the whole earth was of one language, and of one speech." Gen.11:1. {And they worked together for self gratification, not according to God plan, think about too many people and one place trying to lead is not good; just like today, too many people trying to rule over God earth is not good. We are not following God plan today; are we?} "And they said one to another, Go to, let us make brick, and burn them throughly. And they had brick for stone, and slime had they for morter." Gen.11:3. {It's not good trying to out think God. We are leaving God plans and going on with our plans. First of all God say flesh and blood shell not enter into the kingdom of heaven. Always remember the mind is nothing but the devil work shop, if we not following God plans.} "And the Lord came down to see the city and the tower, which the children of men builded." Gen.11:5. {Man will destroy man if God let them. He is coming back to see his earth, will we be ready for him or not?} "And the Lord said, Behold, the people is one, and they have all one language; and this they begin to do: and now nothing will be restrained from them, which they have imagined to do." Gen.11:6. {Man can't handle any power, God gave man power and control over the Garden of Eden, but man could not handle controlling it. But man will not follow God commandments, what do you think about that? Do we believe God is coming back? Will we be ready when He comes? Are we disappointing God?} "Go to, let us go down, and there confound their language, that they may not understand one another's speech." ^{Gen.11:7} {Jesus was right with God when He came down to them, and Jesus will be back soon again are we messing up? Have we been following God plan of faith in all things? Think about it! Are we sure we are passing? Remember we can't stop God plan at anytime, just look at God saying one word and confused their language, are we not following God instruction? Look at God today: He can break up devastation without firing a gun. Think about it. Before we answer how long will God put up with our sinning, are we passing today? Can the Lord count on us for his plan? He is coming back soon. But look at the generations. "Now these are the generations of the sons of Noah, Shem, Ham, and Japheth: and unto them were sons born after the flood."Gen.10:1. {Look at God plan come together.} "The sons of Japheth; was Gomer, and Magog, and Madai, and Javan, and Tubal, and Meshech, and Tiras."Gen.10:2. {Gomer he was the oldest son of Japheth, and the name Magog of a man and a people in the bible: also the second son of Japheth, and Noah grandson. Look Magog may be a comprehensive term "northern barbarian" and the people of Magog are described as skilled horsemen, as its mention in Ezekiel thirty nine and verse fifteen. But was encounter between good and evil as the end of age. But look Gog and Magog is mention in Revelation chapter twenty, verses eight and nine as a symbolize meaning the anti-Christian forces of the world. Think about it! And Madai the third son of Japheth and Noah grandson, he was probably the ancestor of the Medes. Javan is the name of a person, place, town, or trading post in the southern Arabia. It is also mention in the Old Testament. He also was the fourth son of Japheth and the grandson of Noah. The name Tubal is a man name, a country name, or peoples name, mention in the old testament and he also was the fifth son of Japheth, and the grandson of Noah, more is found in Isaiah chapter sixty-six verse nineteen: the name Meshech is mention in two tribes in the old testament and there name was the tribes of Japheth, and the tribes of Shem. He also was the six son of Japheth. The seven son of Japheth was Tiras; nothing else about Tiras is mention in the bible.} "And the sons of Gomer were Ashkenaz, and Riphath, and Togarmah."Gen.10:3. "Now the Lord had said unto Abram, Get thee out of thy country, and from thy kindred, and from thy father's house, unto a land that I will shew thee" Gen.12:1 {sometimes God have too separated us from our family tradition, and have us to move by faith in Him. Will we pass or not? Will we let God down? Just look at Abram! He is about to leaving the security of his father, kindred and country all because he has faith in God. Do we have faith to make a step for God? Remember Abram whole families worship the moon god, but God will not have any god before him.} "And I will make of thee a great nation, and I will bless thee, and make thy name great; and thou shalt be a blessing:"Gen.12:2 {See what God promise, if we obey him and follow his commandments, think about it; for God always have a plan.} "And I will bless them that bless thee, and curse him that curseth thee: and in thee shall all families of the earth be blessed."Gen.12:3{Look at what God is telling Abram; He will bless the one who bless him, in crease in one that crease him, all we have to do is to follow God instructions listen? Do we believe that He will do that for us today?} "So Abram departed, as the Lord had spoken unto him; and Lot went with him: and Abram was seventy and five years old when he departed out of Haran." Gen.12:4. {Just in case we don't understand read the following. Sometime the Lord has to get us from around family, so we can put all our trust in Him. It's always good for a young man to find his own destiny. Remember to keep our self in a way that the Lord can use us at all times. The Lord has a plan for our life; will we be ready? Remember the Lord can't use us if we haven't been through something; we have to prove our self to God that we are really faithful and dependable. Are we following God plan today; can he use us right now? Abram will be tested over and over again will he pass, are we passing our tests? Abram is walking by faith and when he comes out of one test; look! Here comes another test.}

OUT OF ONE TEST AND RIGTH BACK INTO ANOTHER ONE!

Abram came out of one test to find his self right back into another one. Are we passing today? If God call on us for anything at anytime will we need more time? Will we be ready when He calls? Every day we should give think to God. Abram was not perfect but he gave thanks to the Lord for all things. Today are we following God instructions for faith? Look at Abram he is still moving by faith, and giving God the praise, do we ever give thank to God for anything? Are we following his instructions? Are we walking by faith and trusting in God through all things? Look when our time comes will we keep faith in God? Can the Lord really count on us for anything? Jesus says up on this rock I builder my church, Are we passing today? Remember He has a plan at all-time because He is perfect. But keep our faith in God because He will take care of us through all things. Are we going by His plan? Think about it! Are we passing His tests? Abram, and Sarai, does have the same heavenly father. What do we think about Abram is he following God plan? But God is always with us and He never leaves us; just keep our faith in Him. He is our Father; thinks about that} "Say, I pray thee, thou art my sister: that it may be well with me for thy sake; and my soul shall live because of thee."Gen.12:13. {Always trust in God for he has a plan for us at all times, do you trust in God? Remember He have a plan! Always remember God can take your life and give you life, are you following Him today? Remember He know our heart. Sometime the Lord sends us in the enemy camp for a reason, would you pass God test? Are would we talked our self out of doing thing? Look at God power at work for Abram; God is testing him. We may not see Abram passing. God is showing Abram He have all power; just keep faith in Him at all times. Are we following God or following our self? Think about it good before we answer.} "And He entreated Abram well for her sake: and he had sheep, and oxen, and he asses, and menservants, and maidservants, and she asses, and camels."Gen.12:16. {God will never leave us along at anytime. But we never have the faith we need in Him. If we just follow his plan for us, keep the faith and do what we now is right; we will pass. Look if we just wait on God; He will make it alright for us} "And the Lord plagued Pharaoh and his house with great plagues because of Sarai Abram's wife." Gen.12:17. {Just look and trust in God and keep the faith like Abram; look God will fight all Abram battle for him. If we don't keep our faith in God; He will not lift a finger for us. Think about this; do we trust in God? Just look at the Lord fighting our battles. Do you have that faith in God to let him fights your battle? Look at how God plan workout for Abram} "And Pharaoh called Abram, and said, what is this that thou hast done unto me? Why didst thou not tell me that she was thy wife?" Gen.12:18. {Sometime it's good not to volunteer too much information because God have a plan. Sometime God let things happen so He can work them out, so with Him we are all his children: But can He trust us at anytime? It's good today to just listen to God; just remember He have a plan for us in everything He do.} "Why saidst thou, She is my sister? So I might have taken her to me to wife: now therefore behold thy wife, take her and go thy way." Gen.12:19. {Look! when God fight you're battle He will make is know to us, if we have all faith in God, He will make the one that wrong us return back to us. Now Pharaoh Know Sarai is Abram wife, but he also know she it his sister by God, His heavenly father. Look if we have faith in the Lord, He will make all thing right, if we follows all of His instruction.} "And Pharaoh commanded his men concerning him: and they sent him away, and his wife, and all that he had." Gen.12:20. {If we have faith in God, He is all we need, just try him for your self and see. Listen! Throughout these generations we will see a lot of repent tests of our faith. Have we pass any of God tests as of yet? Think about it! Remember don't wait to long God is given us our whole life to get is right. What do we think about how God plan is working for Abram? Look he will work for us if we follow His plan.}

ABRAM HAVE ALL FAITH IN GOD AND HE IS STILL WALKING BY FAITH

Abram faith will be tested again and again. Will we be ready for our tests? Remember our tests is coming whether we are ready are not. Are we following the Lord instruction? Look as Lot and Abram comes to a cross road in life; Will they pass or not? Remember God will test us one day. He will examine our heart; will we pass? And Abram went up out of Egypt, he, and his wife, and all that he had, and Lot with him, into the south."Gen.13:1. {God have a plan for Abram and he loved the Lord with all his heart, but he had to pass God tests; Abram was not a poor man.} "And Abram was very rich in cattle, in silver, and in gold." Gen.13:2. {If we follow God instructions and except God love, He will give us all we need. Look God will make us richer, then our wildest imagination just keep our faith in God; don't let materialistic things come between you and God. Think about it are we passing any of God tests? Look sometime the Lord will take us all around, in a circle to test our faith, and our patience, and bring us back to the beginning. If we will follow God instructions, remember we can pass. Look! Sometime He gives us a second chance, think about it! Time is running out on us but God will bring us back. God is always test us, do we every give think to the Lord for anything? We will have good days and some bad days, but look at Abram gives all think to God for everything at all times. Do we give thinks to the Lord for anything at anytime? Be truthful to our self listen; the Lord will test Lot through Abram. Another test for Abram: wills he pass this time? We support our kindred in there wrong, will Abram support family, over righteousness; what do you think about it? If this happen to us what would we do? God is so good He knows things and further for us; are you leaning to depending on God in all situations?} "And there was strife between the herdmen of Abram's cattle and the herdmen of Lot's cattle: and the Canaanite and the Perizzite dwelled then in the land." **Gen.13:7.** {Abram is put to another test; will he pass? Are will he put family first or do the righteousness thing. Think about this it's just a test for Abram and his faith. Will we put God before our children; think about it as you read below.} "And Abram said unto Lot, Let there be no strife, I pray thee, between me and thee, and between my herdmen and thy herdmen; for we *be* brethren." **Gen.13:8.** {Abram would not want problems in the families' sometime families have two separate, to keep the peace we must make hard decisions.} "Is not the whole land before thee? Separate thyself, I pray thee, from me: if thou wilt take the left hand, then I will go to the right; or if thou depart to the right hand, then I will go to the left." **Gen.13:9.** {Abram is handle the problem good; remember he is in a test from God, sometimes our families can be our worst enemies, don't let anything stand in your way of doing anything for God. Remembers God it always testing our faith; are we passing? Abram, let Lot, took first choice of the best looking of all the land, but remembers sometime the best looking is not always the best for us. But did Lot have the faith he need in God? Lot will be tested now through everything he does for God. But remember everything that looks good is not good, if we just follow God plan we will never go wrong. Are we following God plan for us? Think about it. Just listen to what Jesus is saying.} "He that loveth father or mother more than me is not worthy of me: and he that loveth son or daughter more than me is not worthy of me." **Matt.10:37.** {Remember this is a test for Lot, will he pass are not? They departed on peacefully and good terms, are we today? Do we have that faith in the same God? Are we following God plan for us? But are we making plan for our self? Think about it. Abram loved his brother son Lot, but he loves the Lord more then anything, he don't put anything before the Lord; are we?} "But the men of Sodom were wicked and sinners before the Lord exceedingly." **Gen.13:13.** {If we are not led by God we are headed for troubles in our life, are we following God? Look at Lot, he is headed for one of God tests, for him and his life, will he pass? If we follow God plan for our life, we will be all right; just look at what God is doing for Abram. Do we have the trust in God that we need? Think about it! Remember God own all the land in the world. Look as God tells Abram to keep his faithfulness.} "And I will make thy seed as the dust of the earth: so that if a man can number the dust of the earth, then shall thy seed also be numbered." Gen.13:16. {It's all about our faith; do we have faith in God plan? Are do we have faith in someone else? If God came today would we truly be pass His tests? Think about it, are we ready right now? Are would we need more time? Are would we be ready for His gifts or His love? Are would we be ready for his punishments? Just look and see how good God can be. Think about this: Are we doing what the Lord said? Are we following His plan? Are we passing God tests? Would we like Abram following God instructions? Abram gave thanks to God for a good journey, for his family, and for the food. Abram loved God and follow His plan for him. Are we giving God thanks for all God shares with us today?

WE WILL HAVE MANY UPS AND DOWNS

Abram builder an altar unto the Lord, and called upon His name and gave thank upon the Lord, for taking care of him and his family; read Genesis chapter fourteen. He speaks of the first wars of the kings for power and the nations. {We have wars today over power and oil. Abram won the battle and return Lot back home after he had been captivity. Abram, was blessed by Melchizedek and they recognize Abram to be a bless man of God. God has delivered there enemies into Abram hands. Melchizedek king of Salem; he blessed Abram and gave him tithes of all. Keep your faith in God; He is our shield. Are we waiting on God? Are we trying him for our self? Remember God can't lie to us, but we lie to God ever day. Look! Can God count on us for anything? We must prove our self to God; do we understand? Do we trusts in the Lord? He is all we need to get by. Are we following God instructions, think about it! do we doubt the Lord love for us, are we passing any of the Lord tests today? But Look! How God will bless us if we following his instructions, do we have God in our life now thank before we answer? If we have faith in God and be obedient to Him, He will bless us. The Lord love can't be duplicated what do we think? "After these things the word of the Lord came unto Abram in a vision, saying, Fear not, Abram: I am thy shield, and thy exceeding great reward. Gen.15:1. {Keep your faith in God; He is your shield, are you following the Lord instructions today?} "And Abram said, Lord God, what wilt thou give me, seeing I go childless, and the steward of my house is this Eliezer of Damascus?" Gen.15:2. {Have faith in God and wait on the Lord, are you waiting on Him today?} "And Abram said, Behold, to me thou hast given no seed: and, lo, one born in my house is mine heir. Gen.15:3. {No your heir is coming wait for God plan to come though are you waiting on God today? think look it.} "And, behold, the word of the Lord came unto him, saying, this shall not be thine heir; but he that shall come forth out of thine own bowels shall be thine heir. Gen.15:4. {I will give you your heir from your on bowl, but you much keep the faith in God and wait upon the Lord: Are you today?} "And he brought him forth abroad, and said, look now toward heaven, and tell the stars, if thou be able to number them: and he said unto him, so shall thy seed be." Gen.15:5. {Remember God cannot lie to you; but we lie to God ever day. Can God count on you for anything? We much prove our self to God; do you understand look?} "And he believed in the Lord; and he counted it to him for righteousness." Gen.15:6. {And he was very thankful to God for being so good to him, are you thankful to God for your blessings today?} "And he said unto him, I am the Lord that brought thee out of Ur of the Chaldees, to give thee this land to inherit it." Gen.15:7. {Do you trusts in the Lord? He is all you need to get by, are you following God instructions? Are you passing today? Think about it!} "And he said, Lord God, whereby shall I know that I shall inherit it? Gen."15:8. {Do not doubt the Lord love. Trusts Him in all things, Are you passing any of the Lord tests today? Remember He will test you at anytime.} "In the same day the Lord made a covenant with Abram, saying, Unto thy seed have I given this land, from the river of Egypt unto the great river, the river Euphrates: Gen.15:18. {Look how God will bless you if you following His instructions, Do you have God in your life now? Think before you answer.} "From the wilderness and this Lebanon even unto the great river, the river Euphrates, all the land of the Hittites, and unto the great sea toward the going down of the sun, shall be your coast. Josh.1:4. "The Lord God of heaven, which took me from my father's house, and from the land of my kindred, and which spake unto me, and that sware unto me, saying, Unto thy seed will I give this land; he shall send his angel before thee, and thou shalt take a wife unto my son from thence." Gen.24:7. {If you have faith in God and be obedient to Him; he will bless you.}

SARAI TRY TO HELP GOD FULFILL HIS WORD

{If we don't waiting on God sometime it will cost us in the long run. Are we ready to pay the price for our action? Sarai will go through a test; will she pass? What do we think?} "Now Sarai Abram's wife bare him no children: and she had and handmaid, an Egyptian, whose name was Hagar." Gen.16:1. {Abram wife is beginning her tests; she is not waiting on God, are we waiting on God next move?} "And Sarai said unto Abram, Behold now, the Lord hath restrained me from bearing: I pray thee, go in unto my maid; it may be that I may obtain children by her. And Abram hearkened to the voice of Sarai." Gen.16:2. {Sarai did not have enough trust in God, so she tries to help God fulfill his words. But always remember God does not need our help in anything, because God have a plan for Abram, but remembers it's not time for it to happen; think about it?} "And Sarai Abram's wife took Hagar her maid the Egyptian, after Abram had dwelt ten years in the land of Canaan, and gave her to her husband Abram to be his wife."Gen.16:3. {Remember it's only one qualified to give you a wife; but look at Sarai forcing her maid to marriage Abram so she can have a child for her husband. Are you bringing children into his world today without God plan? Think about it! Are we ready to become a father or mother? Young ladies keep your self holy onto God he will give you a good husband, if you follow God plan for life. Wait before you become pregnant wait upon the Lord; for He have a plan, do we have all faith in God today? Think about it. Hagar was forced to becoming the first surrogate mother.} "And he went in unto Hagar, and she conceived: and when she saw that she had conceived, her mistress was despised in her eyes." Gen.16:4. {Abram disobey God for his wife Sarai; she let God down and so did Abram. Are we letting God down to today? Think about it. There will be a price to pay; can we pay the price? Can we pay the price?} "And Sarai said unto Abram, My wrong be upon thee: I have given my maid into thy bosom; and when she saw that she had conceived, I was despised in her eyes: the Lord judge between me and thee." Gen.16:5. {Sometime we just will not wait on God and mess our child life up, because that was not God plan? Look at Sarai knowing she did wrong and knowing it will cost them both big. Look are we following God plans today? Are we trying to do things God way or our way? Look is we truthful to our self, are we passing any of God tests? See when we do wrong it's hard for us to live with is, because we know in our heart that it was wrong. But remember Abram did wrong also. He didn't follow God plan; like we are doing today. Look it's only a test are we passing? The Lord is always looking out for His children are we passing his tests today? Think about it before we answer. The Lord will be with us if we keep our faith. Sometime things happen to good people for a reason. Always keep our faith in the Lord; He has a plan.} "And the angels of the Lord said unto her, Return to thy mistress, and submit thyself under her hands." Gen.16:9. {God have a plan for her and her son if she just follow His instructions. Look remember God always have a plan if we pass His tests} "And the angel of the Lord said unto her, I will multiply thy seed exceedingly, that it shall not be numbered for multitude." Gen.16:10. {The angels of the Lord said go back for the Lord has a plan for you and the child. Always remember the Lord will take care are you, just try the Lord and see. The Lord is good at all times, He will keep His promise.} "And the angel of the Lord said unto her, Behold, thou art with child, and salt bear a son and salt call his name Ishmael; because the Lord hath heard thy affliction." Gen.16:11. {Look when God have a plan for us just keep our faith in Him when thing get hard. Always remember our help is on the way; always remember that. If we don' follow his instruction we will go wrong. Listen to God as he describes her son to her; is you passing His tests today?} "And he will be a wild man; his hand will be against every man, and every man's hand against him; and he shall dwell in the presence of all his brethren. Gen.16:12. {God know our future before we are born; He will make ready thing that come up in our life. Look she has faith in God; Do we have faith? The Lord did just as the angel had said to her: See what

God can do, if we be faithful. Look at Hagar the first surrogate mother in the world. Are we passing God tests today? Remember Abram was an old man when Ishmael was born. But God have a plan; are we passing?}"And when Abram was ninety years old and nine, the Lord appeared to Abram, and said unto him, I am the Almighty God; walk before me, and be thou perfect." Gen.17:1. {God still have a plan for Abram, he will be tested again and again before he passes God tests of faith, are you passing today? Take a deep breath before you answer? The Lord is telling Abram, what he will do if he just waits on him? Listen to God as he tell Abram; I had a plan for you, but I cannot use that name are Abram anymore. Abram you have disobeyed me I will not blessed the name Abram anymore. God have a plan for the body not the name Abram. The name Abram lost his credibility with God, have you lost your credibility with God? God cannot use the old name Abram, God have give Abram a new name: Abraham. God change his name do you understand, a new start with a new name Abraham will be tested: will he pass? Are we ready for our changes? God couldn't use the name of Abram any more for his plan; we all mess up and make mistakes. But don't wait to long to change. When we mess up ask God to forgive you, if you wait to long and die you will go to hell. Think about that! God promised to Abraham is an everlasting covenant through him, and his sons' generations. Have God ever giving us a second chance, to passing our tests? Think about it! Remember we will see this again. Abraham generations will be tested; will they pass? "This is my covenant, which ye shall keep, between me and you and thy seed after thee; every man child among you shall be circumcised." Gen.17:10. {The first circumcision was a covenant between God and Abraham. But today we must have faith in Jesus, are we keeping our covenant of faith with Jesus today? But remember Jesus purchase us with his blood so it's all about our faith. Are we faithful to Jesus today? Look as Abraham follow instructions from God. God is giving Abraham the instruction that he must do for a covenant with him. Today are we following God instruction like Abraham, please don't be lying to your self or God. Truly are we following all of God commandments? Remember fathers it's our duties to teaching all our children, about what Jesus did for all of us on the cross. God is telling Abraham what he must share the salvation with our children's to in so many words. Today are we doing according to the Lord? Remember what God is saying to Abraham about his descendents; remember this was before Jesus. But remember Jesus purchased us with his blood and put us under grace. God is speaking to the man again not the woman, like God spoke to Adam, but God didn't say anything to Eve, listen to God as he speak to Abraham, what he is about to do. I will change Sarai, name to Sarah God could not use the name of Sarai anymore, but God is giving the name Sarah, a chance to follow His plan with Abraham. God is blessing the name Sarah for she is the wife of Abraham, when God put us together he has a plan for us. Yes as long as we follow God instruction, and pass his tests he will keep on blessing us. Just look at Abraham, he is asking God the wrong thing, that Ishmael be the one he speaks, but listen Abraham don't understand God have a plan for him and Sarah. Listen to God talk to Abraham; listen I will give her a son, but we must wait upon the Lord for he has a plan for us to think about it. God also have a plan for Ishmael because Ishmael is Abraham child. God let things happen for a reason but remember God has a plan. Are we waiting on his plan today, are we remember our tests is coming will we pass are not? Wait on the Lord follows his plan not our, God will do it in His time not our time. But remember we must wait, and not mess up, are we listen to the Lord today? Remember our test is coming are we ready? Just wait on the Lord; He has a plan for us. Are we truly waiting on the Lord today? Just remember it's just a tests; one of Abraham many tests. Abraham did according to the Lord, are we doing this today? Think about it when thing happen in our life. Abraham was and old man when he was doing according to God words, we are never too old to follow the Lord instructions, are we passing? Children obey thy father and live a long life, but Children today rules their father and mother; are we passing? A good father set a good example for his sons; do we set good example for our sons today? Think about it young fathers! Are we following God today?} "And all the men of his house, born in the house, and bought with money of the stranger, were circumcised with him." Gen.17:27. {Abraham is following God instruction; are we? God have a plan for Abraham will he follow his plan? Will we be ready when God messengers shows? When they come will they find you drunk? Are will we be in the wrong places? Think about it before we answer! Remember we will see this again. Remember treat all of God people good at all time: like an angel. We never know when we might be entertaining angels. Will they catch us on a bad day? Remember treat everyone like they are angels. When we are kind to a stranger that make them feel very welcome. Remember God test us in unusual ways; will we be ready when our tests come? Remember God angels don't tell us anything wrong; we do not have to agree with anything that is wrong to keep a friend? If we disagree with thing that is wrong; we will not go to hell. Look at this scripture below it will help us to understand.} "Study to shew thyself approved unto God, a workman that needeth not to be ashamed, rightly dividing the word of truth." Tim.2:15. "And I will give you pastors according to mine heart, which shall feed you with knowledge and understanding."Jer.3:15. "Now Abraham and Sarah were old and well stricken in age; and it ceased to be with Sarah after the manner of women. Gen.18:11. {Always trust the Lord there is nothing impossible for him. The Lord is able to do anything He won't. He made Adam and Eve. He can make any old woman have a child; do we have the faith in God today?} "And the Lord said unto Abraham, Wherefore did Sarah laugh, saying, Shall I of a surety bear a child, which am old?" Gen.18:13. {She does not believe all things are possible for God; you must wait on God plan, are we waiting on God today?} "Is any thing too hard for the Lord? At the time appointed I will return unto thee, according to the time of life, and Sarah shall have a son". Gen.18:14. {God work on his time not our time; we are not the Lord; so we much wait for God plan to work. Are we following God plan today?} "Then Sarah denied, saying, I laughed not; for she was afraid. And he said, nay;

but thou didst laugh." **Gen.18:15.** {But the Lord is no one fool it's not good to lie at any time to the Lord, remember he know when we are lying to Him. The Lord didn't hold anything back from Abraham, are we that faithful to the Lord? Can the Lord depend on us for anything? If we are not following His plan we will go to hell; the Lord promise us. The Lord love Abraham and wouldn't withhold anything from him; do the Lord have that much trusts in us? The angles of the Lord never hold anything back from Abraham. Can they trust us like that today and are we following his plan?} "And the Lord said, because the cry of Sodom and Gomorrah is great, and because their sin is very grievous;" **Gen.18:20.** {Always know that the Lord hears our cry, He will come on his time. Will we be ready when he comes? Remember the Lord will help us only if we are faithful to him? The Lord is checking thing out through his angles, but remember what ever their eyes see and the ears hear so do the Lord, If we don't stop our sinning the Lord will send us to hell. He has that kind of power. Abraham is intercede for the righteous and Sodom, are we righteous enough to intercede for someone? Are we following God plan for us today?} "And Abraham drew near, and said, Wilt thou also destroy the righteous with the wicked?" **Gen.18:23.** {If the righteous remain in the midst of all that wicked yes, because sometime we know it's wrong, but we go along with it anyway but listen to Abraham at he intercede, for Sodom. Abraham loves God people; he is not selfish so he ask God wouldn't he not destroy the city for fifty righteous sake? Listen to God for peradventure if I found fifty, I will not destroy the city. Look Abraham bid down to ten people; can he find ten people today? Ok if you don't find ten but nine yes I would, how you would feel if you weren't numbered nine and a righteous person? Think about it! he was speaking about men, women and children, out of all them together I need ten righteous; but what if ten is not found today? Can He count on you? Think about it} "And the Lord went his way, as soon as he had left communing with Abraham: and Abraham returned unto his place. **Gen.18:33.** {If you are a righteous person you can ask of the Lord anything, and he will grant it for you; try Him and see.} "And there came two angels to Sodom at even; and Lot sat in the gate of Sodom: and Lot seeing them rose up to meet them; and he bowed himself with his face toward the ground;" **Gen.19:1.** {Will we no angels when we see them or would we fail? Are we following God plan at all times? He is checking on us; are we going to pass or will we let him down again.} "And he said, Behold now, my lords, turn in, I pray you, into your servant's house, and tarry all night, and wash your feet, and ye shall rise up early, and go on your way. And they said, nay; but we will abide in the street all night." **Gen.19:2.** {Remember washing of the feet shows great respect. Would we let them into our house or would we turn them away? Remember angels maybe among us today. Tell the true are we going God plan?} "And he pressed upon them greatly; and they turned in unto him, and entered into his house; and he made them a feast, and did bake unleavened bread, and they did eat."**Gen.19:3.** {Would you have fed them? be careful and be truthful to your self. God knows our heart; we will not be able to lie to God. Are would we be like the rich man and Lazarus? Are we passing God tests today? Remember heaven or hell our choice?} "But before they lay down, the men of the city, even the men of Sodom compassed the house round, both old and young, all the people from every quarter: And they called unto Lot, and said unto him, where are the men who came in to thee this night? Bring them out unto us, that we may know them."Gen.19:4-5. {Would we have sent them out Knowing the people of that city? They wanted to have their way with these men: would we have passed the test? That tells me the people of that city was corrupted and was up to no good. But listen if we don't share our life with God on a daily basis, we will get corrupted in sin. The new international version of the bible speaks clearly, these men wanted to have sex with the men. But let's look at what the bible says about homosexuality in the following scripture below} "Thou shalt not lie with mankind, as with womankind: it is abomination." Lev.18:22. {Maybe this scripture will help us to understand a little better.} "If a man also lie with mankind, as he lieth with a woman, both of them have committed abomination: they shall surely be put to death; their blood shall be upon them." Lev.20:13. {This is just a small example scripture from the Old Testament and look at the New Testament examples scriptures.} "For this cause God gave them up unto vile affections: for even their women did change the natural use into that which is against nature:" "And likewise also the men, leaving the natural use of the woman, burned in their lust one toward another; men with men working that which is unseemly, and receiving in themselves that recompense of their error which was meet."Rom.1:26.27. {Remember something's we say and do sometime it can cost.} "Even as Sodom and Gomorrah, and the cities about Gen.19:10. {They in like manner, giving themselves over to fornication, and going after strange flesh, are set forth for an example, suffering the vengeance of eternal fire." Jude.1:7. {Is this your life? If so it's time for a change; you can't lie to God. Think about it! But it will cost you in the long run. "And Lot went out at the door unto them, and shut the door after him,"Gen.19:6. {Lot knew the men were not righteous and is sinners; he knew that they were liars, backstabber, homosexual, murderers, and all kind of people. But! Lot said to his brethren don't search for wicked thing.} "Behold now, I have two daughters which have not known man; let me, I pray you, bring them out unto you, and do ye to them as is good in your eyes: only unto these men do nothing; for therefore came they under the shadow of my roof."Gen.19:8. {Would we put our life no the line to protection strangers? Listen to Lot! he is passing, but the evil and sin in that town is about to overtake Lot. If we let sin go on for a long time is will corrupt us.} "But the men put forth their hand, and pulled Lot into the house to them, and shut to the door." {But Lot is passing his test of love for God; it's so good when we are faith to God. Are we good to the Lord today? Remember he know when we are telling a lie.} "And they smote the men that were at the door of the house with blindness, both small and great: so that they wearied themselves to find the door." Gen.19:11. {Remember the Lord will always be our shield in time of trouble, he will send us what we need. Remember all that was need were ten righteousness'.} "And the men said unto Lot, Hast thou here any besides? Son in law, and thy sons, and thy daughters, and whatsoever thou hast in the city, bring them out of this place:" Gen.19:12. {Look at the Lord given Lot one more chance to get his family out of the city. We need to listen to the angels.} "For we will destroy this place, because the cry of them is waxen great before the face of the Lord; and the Lord hath sent us to destroy it."Gen.19:13. {God is going to destroy that place now because we don't understand how He is.} "I have seen also in the prophets of Jerusalem a horrible thing: they commit adultery, and walk in lies: they strengthen also the hands of evildoers, that none doth return from his wickedness: they are all of them unto me as Sodom, and the inhabitants thereof as Gomorrah."Jer.23:14. "Making them an ensample unto those that after should live ungodly;" 2pet.2:6. "And Lot went out, and spake unto his sons in law, which married his daughters, and said, up, get you out of this place; for the Lord will destroy this city. But he seemed as one that mocked unto his sons in law."Gen.19:14. {Remember Lot has more sons and daughters beside the two that liver with him. Lot has son and son-in-law he also has daughters in law and daughters in the city. Remember all the men in the city will be destroyed with the wicked men, and that included the women's and children's. Remember God gives every body a choice. Sometime the good has to suffer with the bad. But God will take care of his children. God knows the hearts of all his righteous children. Are you following God instructions? Are we passing God tests? Remember called upon the Lord while he is near, for night come when on man can work. If Jesus came today will we go to hell or heaven; think about it.} "And when the morning arose, then the angels hastened Lot, saying, Arise, take thy wife, and thy two daughters, which are here; lest thou be consumed in the iniquity of the city."Gen.19:15. {Do you hear what he is saying? take your wife and your two daughters and leave. This let me know that Lot, his wife and two daughters was not corrupter with sin. But look at the Lord he doesn't discriminate; Lot being the nephew of Abraham was not the reason he was not destroy. The reason Lot was not destroy was because he was faith to the Lord. He didn't let the people corrupter him or make him sin. But remember the people didn't follow God instruction; they didn't pass God test so they was destroy. Are you passing his tests today? He is on his way back; will we be ready when he comes?} "And while he lingered, the men laid hold upon his hand and upon the hand of his wife, and upon the hand of his two daughters; the Lord being merciful unto him: and they brought him forth, and set him without the city."Gen.19:16. {Lot whose following God instruction; are we following the Lord instructions? His angles are already in town. Are you passing God tests, he will be graded every day. Maybe you are not passing today, it's not too late. Do not let your family and friend be the reason you don't follow God instruction and in up in hell. Remember you must be dedicated to God and go alone with his plan.} "Then the Lord rained upon Sodom and upon Gomorrah brimstone and fire from the Lord out of heaven;"Gen.19:24. {In the days of Noah it was water. But now it will be fire like in the days of Solomon and Gomorrah. We have been given a chance; will we get it right today?} "And he overthrew those cities, and all the plain, and all the inhabitants of the cities, and that which grew upon the ground."_{Gen.19:25}. {Think about this: what if we were there and there was only nine righteous. It's not good to be around sinners. If we don't tell them right; we will go to hell. It someone is wrong don't agree with them or hold someone up when you know they are wrong. But look Lot wife was instructed not to look back, but she didn't follow instruction and she looks back and turns into a pillar of salt. Lot and his two daughters was lead through by faith in God. But we have a bad habit of not doing thing we supposed to do. Remember Lot wife thought about it; she has more sons, daughters, brothers and sisters, they were also left back there. It's not good to disobey the rule are God at any time, it can cost us. Lot wife didn't have faith as strong as Lot; how is our faith today? Remember we don't now the hour or day that God comet; we need to be ready at all time, think about it? Remember don't be like Lot wife and let our family cause us to go to hell. If God put us together we will be equally yoked and we will do thing righteousness and God way. Do we have the faith in God, are we passing God test of faith? If God didn't put us two together we will not pass his tests. God will not pass us for doing wrong. Look at Lot as he pass God test. Abraham greatest fear had came true; God didn't find ten righteous people, not even his brother son families. God is looking at us at all times and at all things we do. So before we say anything just remember God see us at all times. God is always fair even if we are not fair with him. We need to give God our best at all time. In our tithe, offerings, and our time. Are we passing God tests today? Remember God have a plan for us, are we following his plan today? Remember sometime we have to let go of the past. Lot wife had more children there; so she look back, and was turned to a pillar of salt; maybe it was a test and she fail. Do we walk by faith or do we love God by faith? Maybe when the first thing that happen bad in our life we seem to forget our faith in God. If anything we should know God and He has a plan. Today are we waiting on God plan for us? Are do we react on our fears and do is wrong. Do not let our fears make us doubt; always keep our faith in God at all times. Look at Lot two daughters driven by fear to sin. Lot two daughters planning to sin; their fear is override their faith. But it is good to stay in control of your mind at all-time. It's a sin to let anything control our mind at anytime. Lot two daughters plan to make their father drink wine and lay with him; not realizing God has a plan. It's not good to let anything control us; Lot two daughters let sin control them. But! Lot did sin also; he let the wine control him. It's not good to let anything control you but God. It does not say whether of not Lot and his two daughters asked for forgiveness before there death. But always remember if we are not going by God plan we are doing wrong. Please say these words from your heart with your mouth "Lord forgive me before I die; I am a sinner, please right now, I love you, thank you Lord Jesus, Amen. Please say these words: But remember always when we die is will be too late. Let's stop today doing thing for our gratification, remember all glory goes to God. Are we doing what is right in the eyes of the Lord? Think about it. But remember God is our final judge, what isn't seen by man is seen by

God. Think about it good! God is the final examine of your life, if He came today how will He judge us?} "And the Lord visited Sarah as he had said, and the Lord did unto Sarah as he had spoken."Gen.21:1. {The Lord will not lie, he always keep his promise. Sometime we forget about God and try to do thing ourselves and not keep the faith in God. Are you one that is not passing God test today? Think about it! God will always keep his promise.} "But, beloved, be not ignorant of this one thing, that one day is with the Lord as a thousand years, and a thousand years as one day." 2Pet.3:8. {Remember God is not about anytime he is time.} "Through faith also Sarah herself received strength to conceive seed, and was delivered of a child when she was past age, because she judged him faithful who had promised." Heb.11:11. {Remember if God say it, it will happen at the promise time.} "And Abraham called the name of his son that was born unto him, whom Sarah bare to him, Isaac."Gen.21:3. {Abraham did according to the words of the Lord and names his son 'as the Lord instructed him. Are we doing as the Lord instruct us today? It will cost us if we aren't. It's time to start following God plan for us today. Remember back this is a covenant between us and God. God had no time table on his plan for us, are we waiting on God today? God have a plan for all of us, will we let him make us happy today? But remember God has no limit on his time to do anything. Remember in God all things are possible. Abraham was proud of his son Isaac, but remembers God said he would give Abraham a son at his time. But if we do not wait on God it will cost us in the long run; are we truly waiting on God plan to work today for us? "And Sarah saw the son of Hagar the Egyptian, which she had born unto Abraham, mocking."Gen.21:9. {Look what goes around comes around. God will call us out, is we waiting on God plan today.} "Wherefore she said unto Abraham, Cast out this bondwoman and her son: for the son of this bondwoman shall not be heir with my son, even with Isaac".Gen.21:10. {What Sarah asked of Abraham was very selfish, but remembers the Lord didn't command Abraham to lie with Hagar. It's not good to listen to anyone but God, always remember God have a plan, it's always better to wait on God plan for us. Are we waiting on God plan today or is we try to do thing our way? Look when thing start to happen in our life maybe it's not what God want us to do. Remember we should have waiting on God plan; think about it! Are we?} "And the thing was very grievous in Abraham's sight because of his son." Gen.21:11. {Look at what happens in life when we do thing our way and not God way. Think about this! When thing start to go wrong in your life: are you waiting on God plan?} "And God said unto Abraham, Let it not be grievous in thy sight because of the lad, and because of thy bondwoman; in all that Sarah hath said unto thee, hearken unto her voice; for in Isaac shall thy seed be called."Gen.21:12. {God said to Abraham remember I told you I would be back? But you hearken to voice of wife and would not wait for me to give you a son? The scripture below will help you to understand} "Humble yourselves therefore under the mighty hand of God, that he may exalt you in due time:" 1Pet.5:6. {Remember God will always take care are his children; just listen. The Lord have a plan he will take care of the lad and the bondwoman because of the promise, look always have faith in God; He will work it out. It is not Ishmael fault because when he was born God have a plan for him: but he was not the promise child of Abraham.} "And Abraham rose up early in the morning, and took bread, and a bottle of water, and gave it unto Hagar putting it on her shoulder, and the child, and sent her away: and she departed, and wandered in the wilderness of Beersheba." Gen.21:14. {The Lord is testing Hagar faith; will she pass her test. God told her he would take care of the lad. Hagar has faith in the Lord. Look at Abraham also realize that God hath power to take care of Ishmael. But! Abraham also realizes that God has the power to take his wife, the power to take Isaac from him, and to take his life if He wanted. Always follow God plan for us and we will not go wrong. And the water was spent in the bottle, and she cast the child under one of the shrubs." Gen.21:15. {The Lord is testing Hagar faith too: He has promised to take care of the lad before he was born. Would you be passing? Are would you be able to think about God promised at that time?} "And she went, and sat her down over against him a good way off, as it were a bowshot: for she said, let me not see the death of the child. And she sat over against him, and lifts up her voice, and wept." Gen.21:16. {Always hold on to our faith never stop always believing in God. Hagar had to make peace with God but she did not want to see her son die. God had giving us a great responsibility to just see after His children, are we today? Look at Hagar as she wept and prayed to the Lord for her son; He will keeps his promise at all time.} "And God heard the voice of the lad; and the angel of God called to Hagar out of heaven, and said unto her, what aileth thee, Hagar? Fear not; for God hath heard the voice of the lad where he is". Gen.21:17. {Hagar has faith! but God move on his time. When we think there is no hope: God will always be right there. He will keep his promised; remember there is nothing too hard for God. Just remember to keep your faith in God your hold life until death. Have you ever been tested in your life and pass by keeping your faith in God?} "Arise, lift up the lad, and hold him in thine hand; for I will make him a great nation." Gen.21:18. {Listen how God hold on to His promise; He has a plan for the lad. God is good all the time. If we keep our faith in Him, He wills hear our pray. Are we passing today?} "And God opened her eyes, and she saw a well of water; and she went, and filled the bottle with water, and gave the lad drink." Gen.21:19. {Look at God! He will make all things ok if we just keep the faith in Him. Are we following God plan today for us? Think about it. Are we passing? The Lord is testing Hagar faith will she pass her test? God told her he would take care of the lad; Hagar has faith in the Lord. "And God was with the lad; and he grew, and dwelt in the wilderness, and became an archer." Gen.21:20. {The lad grew up and God started a nation through the lad as he said are you following God instructions for you today?} "And he dwelt in the wilderness of Paran: and his mother took him a wife out of the land of Egypt. Gen.21:21. {Hagar the Egyptian woman took a wife of her kindred, for her son a wife for Ishmael live and that place call Beersheba near the wall of the water.

ABRAHAM IS GIVING THE TEST OF HIS LIFE

Abraham is giving the test of his life; will he pass? Think about this! This will be the supreme test. Think about your supreme test; are you ready? It's coming! Are you following God plan for your life? God knows the truth, are we telling the truth? He knows your heart; are we worthy of God love and time?}"And it came to pass after these things that God did tempt Abraham, and said unto him, Abraham: and he said, Behold, here I am."Gen.22:1. {Will we be ready when he calls on us? Do you keep yourself available for him at all times? Your test is coming; will you be ready?} "And he said, Take now thy son, thine only son Isaac, whom thou lovest, and get thee into the land of Moriah; and offer him there for a burnt offering upon one of the mountains which I will tell thee of." Gen.22:2. {Will he keeper the faith will he realized God have a plan, what if this was you; would you pass his test today? Abraham wasn't ready for the weight of the world that had just been placed on his shoulders. Can we just imagine how long Abraham night was? No sleep at all that night. Are we doing thing our way? It's not the right way, if it's not the Lord way, it's the wrong way. We can go all our life doing wrong; but one day we will take a test. Will we pass? Make ready for your test! remember God is not a game. Would we have the faith as Abraham had? Think about it before you answer. Remember this is Abraham second biologic son but he is the promise child from God. Abraham Knows not to be unfaith to God: are you passing his tests today?} "And Abraham rose up early in the morning, and saddled his ass, and took two of his young men with him, and Isaac his son, and clave the wood for the burnt offering, and rose up, and went unto the place of which God had told him." Gen.22:3. {Just think about if Sarah has any idea Abraham was going to offering up her son Isaac. Look! Abraham would not be able to handle Sarah. Abraham had all faith that his son would come back. But he also had sense; he knew his wife wouldn't let him take Isaac. So he took two young men with them; just in case Sarah asks too many questions. But he realized God have all power and he realizes God would be with him. And Abraham realizes God have the power to take Isaac, Sarah and his life and sent them to hell; would you passing? Are we following God instructions today?} "Then on the third day Abraham lifted up his eyes, and saw the place afar off."Gen.22:4. {The longest three days of Abraham life, it's like spending three days in hell. Look can you just imagine what was going on in Abraham mind? He was thinking about when he put out Hagar and Ishmael his other son and all the things he had doing wrong in his life. The following scripture below is what will happen when you disobey God.} "Now the Lord had prepared a great fish to swallow up Jonah. And Jonah was in the belly of the fish three days and three nights."Jon.1:17. {A another example are what happened when you disobey God and he give you another chance} "So Jonah arose, and went unto Nineveh, according to the word of the Lord Now Nineveh was an exceeding great city of three days' journey."Jon.3:3. {The Lord will make you do incredibly thing} "And Jonah began to enter into the city a three day journey in one day, and he cried, and said, yet forty days, and Nineveh shall be overthrown." Jon.3:4. {It is not good to do things your way, following God plan for us is best. If not, look! It can cost you. Just think about if Sarah has any idea where Abraham was going. She would have doing anything to stop Abraham; He would not be able to handle her.} "And Abraham said unto his young men, Abide ye here with the ass; and I and the lad will go yonder and worship, and come again to you. Gen."22:5. {Listen to Abraham faith as he said they would be back; do we have that faith? Think about it! Would we be really to pass the test today? Are we following God instructions?} "And Abraham took the wood of the burnt offering, and laid is upon Isaac his son; and he took the fire in his hand, and a knife; and they went both of them together."Gen.22:6. {Look at Isaac caring his cross like Jesus; are you putting your cross upon you today? If not we need to start to follow God and passing his tests of faith. Look at the example scripture to help you to understand.} "And he bearing his cross went forth into a place called the place of a skull, which is called in the Hebrew Golgotha:" John.19:17. "And Isaac spake unto Abraham his father, and said, my father: and he said, here am I, my son. And he said behold the fire and the wood: but where is the lamb for a burnt offering? Gen.22:7. {Listen to Abraham faith in God; do you understand Abraham faith is unbelievable? Remember Jesus carry his sacrifice crossed.} "And Abraham said, my son, God will provide himself a lamb for a burnt offering: so they went both of them together." Gen.22:8. {Abraham had to reinforce his son faith in God that he would provide? Would we have that faith?} "And they came to the place which God had told him of; and Abraham built an altar there, and laid the wood in order, and bound Isaac his son, and laid him on the altar upon the wood." Gen.22:9. {Remember Abraham is an old man look at Isaac passing his test. Isaac obeyed his father for now; he knows he is the lamb. Would you passing? Here is an example scripture to help you to understand: Remember what the Ten Commandments say.} "Honor thy father and thy mother: that thy days may be long upon the land which the Lord thy God giveth thee." Exo.20:12. {If we keep this in our heart we will not go wrong we will pass God tests.} "And Abraham stretched forth his hand, and took the knife to slay his son." Gen.22:10. {Look at Abraham passing God test of faith. Are we passing today, can God count on us remember God will test us, with something we love are some one we love; will we pass today? Remember God know us long before we knew our self.} "And the angel of the Lord called unto him out of heaven, and said, Abraham, Abraham: and he said, here am I." Gen.22:11. {Abraham has passing God tests of faith and Isaac had pass God test, are we passing his tests today and are we ready? Listing to the angel from heaven calls out to Abraham; listing to God angel} "And he said, lay not thine hand upon the lad, neither do thou any thing unto him: for now I know that thou fearest God, seeing thou hast not withheld thy son, thine only son from me." Gen.22:12. {Abraham was very relieved and very happy because he had pass God test of faith. Abraham was a man of God and he didn't give up. God is given Abraham a sound charge. Will you pass if God given you sounds charge? Are we passing our tests? Look at God come through for Abraham He will come though for us.} "And Abraham lifted up his eyes, and looked, and behold behind him a ram caught in a thicket by his horns: and Abraham went and took the ram, and offered him up for a burnt offering in the stead of his son."Gen.22:13. {God will provide for us with a ram just as he did for Abraham. Do we understand what God is saying, if we keep our faith in him and follow His instructions. What if we had to prove our faith to God today; would we pass? Remember if we are doing wrong God will call us out someday; will we be ready? Abraham remembers all things he had done in his life wrong and he asked the Lord to forgive him. Have we ever asked God to forgive us for doing the wrong things in our life? Will we pass the big test of God and will we be ready? Abraham faith was tested and restored; God will always supply your need by faith; do we have all faith in God today.} "And the angel of the Lord called unto Abraham out of heaven the second time," Gen.22:15. {And God said to Abraham you have not withheld your only son from me. Listen I will greatly multiply your seed as the stars in heaven and as the sand is up on the sea. He is also saying as long as Abraham be obedient to his voice and be faithful he will make nations of his seed. "And God was with the lad; and he grew, and dwelt in the wilderness, and became an archer." Gen.21:20. {The lad grew up and God started a nation through the lad as he said; are you following God instructions today?} Look these example scriptures are for us to understand better, God is testing us everyday are you passing? Judah had married a Canaanite woman so he found a Canaanite wife for his firstborn son. The Lord gives us time after time to get things right. If we keep doing wrong the Lord will take us out of this word. Are we passing his test today? "And Er, Judah's firstborn, was wicked in the sight of the Lord; and the Lord slew him." "And Judah said unto Onan, Go in unto thy brother's wife, and marry her, and rise up seed to thy brother." Gen.38:7-8. {The Lord didn't judge the Canaanite woman but Tamar for the wicked of Judah firstborn son Er. In order to maintain the family blood line the next single brother would marry the widow and keep the blood line. Remember some things we do in life fall down to our children. Our sin again the Lord will cost us. But look what happened when we stop following instructions from the Lord.} "And Onan knew that the seed should not be his; and it came to pass, when he went in unto his brother's wife, that he spilled it on the ground, lest that he should give seed to his brother." Gen.38:9. {This is the first record of a waste of a life in the world, as of today we call it abortion and it was done by a man. Punishment for the waste of life was done by the Lord. Remember the Lord say be fruitful and multiply and to replens the earth with life not to take away. Because of his own selfishness and wicked he didn't conceive a child with his brother widow. But remember two men can't reproduce or two women can't reproduce; think about it. Are we following the Lord instructions today? Are we passing his test of faith? Remember God it the final judge? The bible said we anger God, do we think we are pleasing God? "And the thing which he did displeased the Lord: wherefore he slew him also." Gen.38:10. {Today are we doing thing that displeasing to the Lord? think about it! are we following the Lord instruction today? remember we can lie to our self but not too God. Remember we can hide from man but not from God. Just remember! Think about God; He is getting tried of our sin. The Lord judged Onan just as he judged us.} "Then said Judah to Tamar his daughter in law, Remain a widow at thy father's house, till Shelah my son be grown: for he said, lest peradventure he die also, as his brethren did. And Tamar went and dwelt in her father's house." Gen.38:11. {It was the custom of that day that when a brother dies his brother was to marry his widow. But on the death of Onan she would to go to her father until the younger son is ready for marriage but look what the scriptures below said.} "And in process of time the daughter of Shuah Judah's wife died; and Judah was comforted, and went up unto his sheepshearers to Timnath, he and his friend Hirah the Adullamite." "And it was told Tamar, saying, Behold thy father in law goeth up to Timnath to shear his sheep." Gen.38:12-13. {Apparently this deal that Judah had which concerned seeing this adullamite by the name of Hirad was in connection with sheep. Judah goes up there to shear them in the mean time Tamar has been waiting all this while at home for Judah to give Shelah to her as her husband; but look!} "And she put her widow's garments off from her, and covered her with a vail, and wrapped herself, and sat in an open place, which is by the way to Timnath; for she saw that Shelah was grown, and she was not given unto him to wife." "When Judah saw her, he thought her to be a harlot; because she had covered her face." Gen.38:14-15. {Look at God goes to work the third son of Judah Tamar sees that Judah doesn't intend to give her to his son as his wife so she takes action. She takes off her widow clothes and sits by the wayside with her face covered as was the custom of harlots. Look at God he always do thing that we can't understand. But just remember Jesus and the woman at the well he uses her to get messengers to all the men in the city. Because he knows the men of the city would list to her. Look what go around come around; do we see it in these scriptures? pay attention now.} "And he turned unto her by the way, and said, go to, I pray thee, let me come in unto thee; for he knew not that she was his daughter in law. And she said, what wilt thou give me, that thou mayest come in unto me?" "And he said, I will send thee a kid from the flock. And she said, Wilt thou give me a pledge, till thou send it?" "And he said, what pledge shall I give thee? And she said, Thy signet, and thy bracelets, and thy staff that is in thine hand. And he gave it her, and came in unto her, and she conceived by him." Gen.38:16-18. {Look at the Lord goes to work and what goes around comes around. Look at God! How he work thing out; at all times. But the bracelets were worn by men to indicate their position in life. Look he carried a staff with his mark on it; some things we do in the dark come back and bite us in the light.} "And she arose, and went away, and lay by her vail from her, and put on the garments of her widowhood." Gen.38:19. {Now his daughter in law had to do is wait for God next move; she had following God instruction. Now she has to wait on God.} "And Judah sent the kid by the hand of his friend the Adullamite, to receive his pledge from the woman's hand: but he found her not." Gen.38:20. {But remember what done in the dark will come to light. Remember God is the light of the world. So he will see all things that man sees. The Lord will call us out when we don't follow his instruction.} "Then he asked the men of that place, saying, where is the harlot, that was openly by the way side? And they said, there was no harlot in this place." Gen.38:21. {The Lord works so good he makes us think we are crazy sometime; we can't lie to God and getaway with it. Have we been lying to God and thinking we have got away with it?} "And he returned to Judah, and said, I cannot find her; and also the men of the place said, that there was no harlot in this place." Gen.38:22. {When the Lord Starts to work on us sometime we can't understand what is going on. But when we follow the Lord instruction we don't have to worry about things going on in our life. Are we faithful to God today? Just look at the following scriptures and tell me what you think? "And Judah said, Let her take it to her, lest we be shamed: behold, I sent this kid, and thou had not found her. And it came to pass about three months after, that it was told Judah, saying, Tamar thy daughter in law hath played the harlot; and also, behold, she is with child by whoredom. And Judah said, bring her forth, and let her be burnt." "When she was brought forth, she sent to her father in law, saying, By the man, whose these are, am I with child: and she said, Discern, I pray thee, whose are these, the signet, and bracelets, and staff."Gen.38:23-25. {When we do thing again the Lord will he will call us out on it. Lying to God can hurt to the bone; are we lying to God today? Think about it. The Lord Knowles our name and he will be revealing it soon; have we been doing thing in the dark? Now it will come to the light. Are we passing his tests today? Are we following all of his instruction for us in our life? Yes or no just remember he will call you out.} "Judah acknowledged them, and said, She hath been more righteous than I; because that I gave her not to Shelah my son. And he knew her again no more." Gen.38:26. {The Lord reminds them both of there sins of doing wrong and not following his commandment. Have we recognized in our mind things we are doing wrong today? Do we think we are doing according to God instructions are we passing his tests? Think about it?}

PREPARATION

{I repeat I can't stress this enough! Preachers are we preaching God's words, or are we preaching for our on gratification. Did God call us or did we just go and preach without being called by God; think about it? The wrong answer could cost you your life. So peoples if we are playing with God it's time to stop. Abraham made preparation for his family body after death. Remember don't let the last thing we do in this world is leave our family in debt. Have we already make predations for our death look at Abraham.} "And when Jacob had made an end of commanding his sons, he gathered up his feet into the bed, and yielded up the ghost, and was gathered unto his people." Gen.49:33. {But look Abraham have made all preparation for his day! have we made our preparation for our day? Its coming will we be ready or not? Look we will die! Think about it.} "And Joseph commanded his servants the physicians to embalm his father and the physicians embalmed Israel."Gen.50:2. {This was the first mention of physicians embalming that was done in this world. It was preformed in the book of Israel. Do we really care about our responsibility for our body, just remember Jesus said the body is a temple, are we doing what right for our temple. God will know if we is lying. Have we made the preparation for our body? Think about is before you answer. Now after seeing all these examples does this remind us of anyone, just think about it! Are we passing? Death will come when we least expect it, think about it good now because death it coming; will we be ready? Remember the way we live our life will determine the way we will die, all we have read and all we been through; have we make any kind of change for the best in our life? These entire examples stop know! Have we asked God to forgive us for our sins! It's impossible for anyone to be able to judge your live. God is the final judge; not us. Think about it! Glade we are not the one.}

IT'S TIME FOR A CHANGE

It's time for a change we have came from our birth to now by God grace, are we passing? Remember God is still working on us because of the love he have for us; its time for a change. Are we still lying to God and our self? It's time for a change stop living behind lies; God knows all our needs. Along the way we just may learn more about Him; remember all we have been read, think about this! We put everything before God is we passing today? Remember that God is a jealous God and He will not have no other God before Him. What God has for us is for us! It's time for a change. Remember money is not everything, it's time for a change; it's not about us it all about God. It's time for a change we don't preach God words anymore, are we passing today? We need to preach for God not for fables! think about it are we passing God tests. Preacher for the record let not be ignorant of God righteousness: remember he know when we are lying. We need to stop listen to what people are saying to us and start to read our Bible more. Look God is getting tried of man wicked ways are we the one he it getting tied of? Just think of who we think about besides our self. It's time for a change, think about what we have read. One thing about God he gives everyone there appointed time; are we passing? Who will be there for us besides God! Remember now is the appointed time. Today are we the one that is not passing God little simple tests in life? Remember we will be tested; will we ready or not? It's all about the words of God, not about our status in life, the way we sound or how pretty we hold our mouth. It's all about God words; are we listen to God words today? It's not about our singing it's all about God words; Are we faithful to God today? It's not about the car you driver, it's all about God words, It's not our voice, it's all about God words! Are we passing? Look deacons remember you don't own God church, the pastor appointed you as deacon to help him to attend to God church business and to the widows as need. Deacons think about it today! Are we passing? Remember God tell us he is on his way back! Will we be ready? But pastors! We can be remove if we are not following God words set up in the bible. Also by not living up to what God appointed us for, think about it! Are you passing today? Remember God expectations for is very high. God is not a lukewarm God. Members remember we don't own God church because you paid the more in tithes; remember God made it possible for us to be able to pay our tithes. I repeat people we don't own God church; He gave us an ambassador to be our overseeing of the church for Him and to make right choice. But remember for every action there is a reacting; think about that! Are we passing God tests? Always remember it's your choice hell or heaven.

FINALLY! BROTHERS LISTEN

Remember though is all after reading this book everyone is not going to heaven. So this is why God made hell. But remember no matter how much someone go though; they will not choose to follow God. Remember God is giving us test after test so it's possible to passing God tests. Look we know what God is asking of us, are we ready to follow after God today? Our choice heaven or hell. I am one example out of a trillion people that the Lord blesses in a very special way, but remember we all of God children; but we much learn to obey the Lord; Are we? Remember God is given us a blessing every minute every second of our life are we faithful to Him today? Remember all we need to do is to obey him, and become a living testimony of how good God really is. But sometime He will send us through something to get our attention. It's all about obeying God today. But we are complaining about everything! The Lord has blessed us with everything today? But are we lusting after someone else blessing and blocking our blessing? Because of our greed, because God have a plan for us, before we were formed in our mother womb. Remember though it all after reading this book, everyone shall have a better understands of what God is asking of us. Remember knowing it's up to us heaven or hell. Please make the right choice. But remember no matter how much we go though; we still have a choice. We can follow God and go to heaven or follow the devil and go to hell! Our choice; think about it! Remember God and you are the only one that knows if you are passing. So remember all we have read no one down here is perfect. But we don't know if someone asks God to forgive them before they died, but we do know Jesus was perfect because the Bible and this book say so. But remember always strive to do the best you can. We can start to ask God to forgive us for our down falls. If we think about yesterday; did anything happen in our life that we should give thank to God? Now! Are we following God instruction? Think about it before we answer. Always remember God know our heart. Always remember God love us enough to send us where we desire.

THE END

NOTES AND REFLECTION

NOTES AND REFLECTION

About the Author

My name is Reverend Frank Charleston Jr. I was born to the late Frank Charleston Sr. and Mrs. Annie Mae Lewis Charleston Mullen. I am the oldest of eight children. My parents had six boys and two girls. In April two thousand and three God called the oldest girls home. June twenty-second nineteen eighty-five I marriage the love of my life: Terrie Evon Poellnitz Charleston. We have three young men; they are Donald (LaDawna) Charleston, Marco Charleston and Jason Graham-Charleston. We have four grandchildren; Bria, Taylor, Donald Jr. and Bryce Charleston. I'm the pastor of Christ Blessed Church located at 406 East Monroe Street, Demopolis, Alabama. I attend John Essex High School and graduate in nineteen seventy-three. I had a massive stroke February 25, 2008. I was in a coma for about six week. During that time the Lord was talking with me and I had no choice but to listen. God gave me instructions of how He wanted things to go.

Printed in the United States
By Bookmasters